Praise

"Xue Di's poetry is marked by an alert intelligence and a quiet authority. His work combines composure with force, lyric sensitivity with an expansive sense of scale. Rooted in attentiveness to the material world, these poems achieve resonance through precision rather than excess, offering a measured gravity rare in contemporary verse." —Tang Ming

雪迪诗歌，在机敏中，以睿智的书写，而具备了一个优异诗人所拥有的沉稳、遒劲、苍郁、雄阔和练达厚重。——唐明

"Xue Di's poems are flamboyant, full of images, direct in their emotion, full of personal anguish but exuberantly sensual." —Keith Waldrop, 2009 National Book Award winner

雪迪的诗如同火焰。它们意象丰富,深蓄情感; 充满个人的剧痛,又饱含官能的体验。
科斯·沃尔卓伯,美国布朗大学英语系教授(2009 美国国家图书奖获得者)

"Quiet in tone and intimate in stance, Xue Di's poetry listens its way toward the world. Through finely textured language and a depth of vision that tempers melancholy, his poems reveal how honest speech reconciles finite life with infinite time — and offers solace to human fragility."
—Lu Xiake

雪迪的诗，有着静谧的调子，他善于聆听，以俯身姿态，贴近泥土，草木，一切琐碎的事物发出的声音，以求融入，并抵达它们的频率产生共振。他的文字肌理细腻，感性，略带怅惘，但镜头的纵深感，又抵消了一部分伤感元素，其中的有限生命对无限时空的妥协解构，让我们体味到真诚叙说对于脆弱生命的慰藉。——鲁侠客

"Reading Xue Di's poetry, one is often reminded of Hölderlin — the poet Heidegger once called the poet of poets. Yet the resemblance is paradoxical rather than direct. Unlike classical Romanticism, Xue Di's work is infused with modern sensibility, where realism and conceptual depth coexist. In this sense, his poetry opens a broader horizon for contemporary poetic practice."
—Yanzhi Molly

读诗人雪迪的诗，笔者总是会想到德国诗人荷尔德林，这位被存在主义哲学家海德格尔称为诗人中的诗人。但是，事实上他们是不一样的，更像是一种悖论，相比于古典的浪漫主义，雪迪的诗歌里融入了现代性元素和审美，写实性、观念性具在，从另一方面说，雪迪为当代诗歌呈现了一个更为广阔的写作空间。——胭脂茉莉

BLUE WHITE WATER
蓝色白色的水

BLUE WHITE WATER

蓝色白色的水

by

XUE DI

雪迪

TRANSLATED FROM THE CHINESE
BY ALISON M. FRIEDMAN

译文方美昂

Poetose

Paperback ISBN: 978-1-64672-404-8

eBook ISBN: 978-1-64672-375-1

LCCN: 2026943766

Published by Poetose

Boston, MA

Cover art: "Fractures of Light and Passage" by Ardiansyah A

First Edition

www.poetose.com

BLUE WHITE WATER

蓝色白色的水

一

你站在绿色的草地上，你在唱歌。那
只歌擦过身边，我的胸口一阵阵疼痛。我
不由得弯下身体。那天阳光特别好，在我
脸下勾出明亮的影子。我闻见草的气味。
那天是我们相识的日子。

那天的果园幽暗，神秘。我重新走进
熟悉的地方。交叉小径使我模糊地记起一
些杂乱的梦。许多鸟的声音从园子深处传
来，你的歌也在我的深处，那座心灵的园
子里飞出飞进。你被阳光照出一小团光亮
的脸。那是一个午后，我们相遇的日子的
午后。

静静地读你的脸，略显苍白。歌声去
的很远了，草地逐渐变成深绿色。你隐在
一群女伴中间。四月！在这颗茂密的果树
前，大自然袒露一切：草坪，花；远处那
支发白的河流；坡底的阴影。太阳像灯笼
一样在前方点燃。我竭力回忆你脸中的所
有细节，眼睛眨动时的一段段文字。在所
有流畅和清晰的地方，成为一片空白。突
然，我看见一处错字的地方，我看见"悲
哀"，我看见你的眼帘无声地放下。我们的
命运在这个片刻决定了。

那是在阳光显得明亮的草地上。那是
在四月，我们相识的日子。

You stood in jade fields, singing. Your song grazed my body. In my chest, pain burst; I doubled over. That day, sunlight, bright shadows outlining my face. I smelled the grass, and then I smelled you.

That day, in a creeping orchard — again I find myself here. Crisscrossing paths lead me to forgotten dreams. Bird calls spread over the garden; your song resounds in me, in and out of my heart's garden, your song flies in and out. Our first afternoon, your face in a ring of sun.

I read your paling face lost among eaves. (Your song, spreading, then away. Grassland deepened green.) April's everything before this dense orchard: lawn, flowers, whitening river branch, hillside shade. Sun ignites, a lantern for it all. I exhaust myself for details of your face — in each blink, a new paragraph. All articulate places, now blank space. Wait, a typo: "sorrow." Your eyelids close, seal what will be ours.

On the sunlit field. In April. We.

二

这是雨夜。一个细雨朦朦，路街上铺着湿润的黄缎子的夜晚。哦，我想让你和我一起走走。

随便走走。影子掉在水里，掉进光里摔成了碎片。那些骑车人贴着我们身子，孤零零向前骑去。路灯安静极了，和雨水一同向远方伸展。也许已经很晚了，街上没有人。你只要默默地和我一起走走，这样的夜晚，什么话也不用说。

脸上感到一粒一粒的冰凉。一种"纯"的感受也是这样一粒一粒的掉在心上。那条黄缎子一直铺进远处的黑暗。我的心进入在你肩头生长的黑色的森林里。

影子静静的。在光的上面不停地闪烁。

记住这次欢乐！这次被雨夜融解的欢乐。有那么一个晚上，我们对这个世界曾经相信过！

II

Rain tonight. Night's damp satin spreads over the street. Shall we?

As we please. Shadows trip into watery light, shattering. On bicycles they brush past our bodies and ride forward, alone. Streetlight glow stretches with rain into distance. Already late, no one on the street. Shall we? Silently.

Your face drop by drop turns cold. Onto my heart, "purity." That strip of yellow satin unfurls ahead, a carpet into distant darkness. I enter dark forest grown on your shoulders.

Shadows, quiet. In front of light they don't stop glistening.

Remember this! Melted by rainy night. Then, we had faith in this world.

三

　　再弹一支曲子，再拨一次紧绷在生命里的弦，过去的年龄颤动。未来的幻想迸溅向四面八方。你要求我，寂静中，再弹一次，你眼中闪闪发亮的是什么？

　　我把脸完全埋进，那只被光芒烧破的灯罩。我的心在残破的阴影里。这一切多么熟悉，熟悉的我可以闻出它的味道，熟悉的我浑身颤抖！你用湿湿的手抓住我。告诉我！你眼中闪闪发光的是什么？

　　儿时母亲哼歌时呼出的气是湿湿的。母亲讲故事时，眼中也这样闪闪发亮。这一切多么遥远了，记忆的岛早已下沉。如今那里一片汪洋。如今我孤身前来。在生命最黑暗的地点仍有一条闲置的船，为了在有月亮的晚上能够重新漂流在那块水面上。告诉我！在我对这一切都无比熟悉的时候，你的要求，漂动在黑暗里的眼睛，你眼睛里漂流的光，光上的潮湿，那只抓住我，使我感觉疼痛的手，这一切！对你，对我，意味着什么？

　　别说。什么也别说。

III

Another song, please. Pluck each string, taut across our living, each quivering year gone by. Tomorrow's illusion bursts in all directions. You demand, in silence, play another. (What glimmer, in your eyes?)

My face under light, lamp burned. My heart in wretched shadow. So familiar, I can smell its flavor, so familiar, from head to toe trembling. Your moist hand grasping me. Tell me! What glimmer in your eyes?

I, a child, and mother humming; damp breath. Telling stories, in her eyes also this glimmer. Now, so distant. Memory's island already sunk. Now, vast water and alone. In darkest corner a waiting boat, to be driven by current under moon, across surface. Tell me! When all is familiar, your demands, your eyes in darkness, light in your eyes, wet light seizing me, hands of pain, all of this! For you, for me, what does it mean?

Don't. Don't say a word.

四

  那天我坐在屋子里想，我为什么会爱上你？谁把你领到我的面前，把我像一颗球似的弹向你，与你相撞；留下纷纷飞溅的幸福的痛苦，留下一块块想念你的疤痕。那天屋子外面下雨，雨水在窗玻璃外面流，屋子里是灯光，摇摇曳曳，沿着窗玻璃蹒跚。雨水和灯光隔着一层玻璃，亲爱的，像一只碧绿透明的眼睛隔着一块土地向另一个世界窥探。灯光和我隔着柔软的膜，我坐在屋子角落里想你。哦，你也想我吧，当然，你可以不告诉我，我与你被一层东西阻断。是的，我曾紧紧地抱住你，吻你，像我摊开四肢向着一座森林躺下，像我轻轻抚摸自己的皮肤。但，亲爱的，我们之间被一个可以无限扩大的点隔开。在我们紧紧相抱时它隐藏在身体之间。它被我们的热情挤压得很小，但它存在着！

  亲爱的，你不知道幸福也是一种痛苦吗？如果我生活在持续的苦难之中，幸福将像一道强光使我在瞬间晕眩。持续的苦难造成一种抵抗的力，幸福会使它骤然弯曲，反弹回来以至伤害自己。

IV

In the room, thinking. Why love, why you? Who bounced me toward you like a ball? Gleeful sorrows, splattering one after another. Scars remind me of you. That day, rainwater along the window pane, lamplight flirting and staggering along glass. Between rainwater and lamplight, a pane of glass, like land between a dark green transparent eye and a world beyond. Lamplight kept from me by a delicate membrane; I sit in the corner of your absence. You miss me; you won't tell me; you and I too, separated by a layer. I have held you, kissed you, like limbs unfurled, prone before forest; like stroking my own skin. An infinitely expanding point, smothered and small by our bodies, now darling, it grows.

Happiness, a kind of suffering? In continuous misery, joy bursts violent, unglues me. Continuous sorrow like resin, but happiness curves it against me.

四续

　　但，亲爱的，你还要抱着我，吻我，把你湿漉漉的嘴唇辗过我干燥的皱纹的街道。只是当我站在阳光下睁不开眼的时候，别笑话我，或诅咒我。当我把你的目光一根根绕在我手指上，别去逼问我为什么沉默不语。亲爱的，让我现在就告诉你。我在想：

　　我们究竟是被一只什么样的手拨弄？在什么样的距离，我们能够逃避手掌翻动的速度？什么样的地点，我们能够步入天国？

IV CONT.

    Still embrace me, kiss me, trace your wet lips along arid lines in my face. When I stand in sunshine and cannot open my eyes, don't laugh, don't curse me. When I wind your gaze strand by strand around my fingers, don't ask me why silence. Now let me:

    What kind of hand, after all, tosses fate? And how escape the reaching palm? Where enter Heaven?

五

每次你用这种眼神看我，我就感觉有一只手开始撕我的皮肤，一种不堪忍受的寂静，把我的眼，耳和所有器官，死死裹住。印第安猎手在草坡上，注视用垂死的眼睛钉住他的猎物。

我是猎物！在"爱情"这场角逐中，我浑身沐浴阳光，两眼苍白。四面是绿茵的草场，天空蔚蓝。当贴着草地飞来一支忧郁忍耐的目光，我被射中。我的身体蜷缩在草里，像一只被丢弃的皮毛掉光的鼓。

每次你用这种眼神看我，我见到爱的荒凉的林子。我见到你，纯洁，褴褛而瘦小的朝圣者。

我是一只击声沉闷的鼓。

V

Each time that expression in your eyes: a hand tearing my skin, silence smothering my eyes, my ears, my entrails. A hunter on the sloping field stares at his prey staring back at him with dying eyes.

I am prey! In amorous chase, under sun, my eyes, pallid still. All directions, green fields and azure sky. Shot by your gaze, melancholy patience, across land like an arrow. My body curls up on the grass, hairless pummeled skin of an abandoned drum.

Each time, that expression in your eyes, love's barren forest. You, a withered pilgrim.

I am a drum, dulled.

六

现在你在干什么？在夜的那一边。

这是夜晚。这是我和你相距那样遥远的夜晚。这是一块黑布，把心弹向高处，体会掉落时四周的空无和恐怖。

我躺在夜晚柔软的黑缎子上。四周是你星星一样闪烁的面孔。

我赤裸，赤裸得有如裹着一圈又一圈的麻布。它使我禁不住用手指去按我的心，在我的喉咙里发出嘶哑的声音。又一次我孑然一身了。又一次！我被紫丁香和星星包围，然后被清脆的声音弹出，眼窝像烧破的灯笼，摇晃在月亮下。赤裸，赤裸得那么沉重。四周是你惊起的夜鸟般的叹息。

在夜的那一边，你在干什么？

我想象不出来。你经历的是我无法想象的。你的周围是一个个被掠夺得干干净净的日子，在寂静的苦难中，你的脸灿然开放，承接着清晨的露水。谁也不要去抵抗命运，谁也不要在西南风横扫大地时，在抗争中把自己弄的光秃秃的。光秃，而且干躁，感觉我在遥远的另一边洒下的无用的泪水。

VI

What are you doing, there in night?

This. The night of our distance. This black cloth, tossing my heart; falling, only horror, then empty.

I rest on night's supple dark satin. All around me your face glitters like stars.

Unsheltered me, bound in rounds of linen. Can't stop reaching for my heart, reaching fingers. Voice, hoarse in my throat. Again alone. Again! Enveloped in lilac and stars, startled by a clear voice. Eye sockets sway, cracked lanterns below the moon. Naked, naked and so heavy. All around your sighs startle night birds.

Somewhere else, what, in night, do you do?

I cannot. I cannot fathom your nights. All around you, days robbed clean; silent in suffering, your face still opens, held out to catch morning dew. No one should resist fate; no one left like trees, leaf-stripped after southwest wind. Bare and dry, I feel my tears in vain there.

六续

黑夜会在一个边缘连接。那时我与你再度相逢。在我们头顶向前的第三颗星星，射出淡淡的光辉，我仍旧想知道，那时，你想的，做的是什么？

面孔。你的面孔在我梦中，像鱼一样游来游去。

VI CONT.

Night blurs edges. There, we can return.
Our heads face a third star, radiant. Tell me,
there, what will you think, and do?

Your face in my dreams, a fish swimming
back and forth.

七

　　可是这个早晨呢？昨夜下的霄还没有融化。那些雪横卧在枝杈上，它使我想到你的悲哀；冰凉的，洁白的，覆盖在我身上。

　　脚下的路湿湿的。你的梦？昨夜雪花飘下时的梦。昨夜，玻璃发出响声。

　　纷乱的枝条承接着雪，承接像雪一样纷纷飘下的东西。那些屋顶，山和原野，被光线穿插的空气；平坦，裸露的部位，暗中怀着焦渴的愿望。

　　我慢慢地在这个早晨里行走。两旁缀满了雪的树枝环绕的街，寂静无人的片刻，能维持多久？使我的心骚乱不安的一切，能维持多久？雪在枝头消融，化成水一滴滴掉落的意象倒比这条街的意象更鲜明，更有力地打进我的心。它的暗示将尾随我的一生。

　　这个早晨，我感到你的悲哀。冰凉的，洁白的，覆盖在我的身上。

VII

This morning? Still, last night's snow, prone on branches; your frozen sorrow, spotless, blanketing my body.

Road damp beneath my feet. Your dream? Last night during snowflakes. Last night, glass produced sound.

Branches helter-skelter catch snow, catch things cascading like snow. Roofs, mountains and fields, light-sliced air, flat and exposed; inside, thirst desires.

I drag through this morning. Street lined with snow branches, people-less quiet, how long...? Tormenting me, how long...? Snow disappears from branches. Trickling water, more glistening than this street, beats drop by drop onto my heart. It whispers: I will follow 'til your end.

This morning, your frozen sorrow, spotless, blanketing my body.

八

　　这是你送我的照片。这是我们相爱的证明。

　　爱过，被沉重的黄土埋葬过。我的心在你的注视下发过芽，当你在六月的天空里向我走来时结成果实，炫耀在枝头。鸟的细细的爪子挠着；雨和小小的河水，招呼我，做些湿湿的梦。

　　你的照片插在我的前方。这是果实累累的果园。

　　爱过，被爱的车子飞快地拦腰辗压过。今天再一次在大地上走动，看见纷纷飞起的尘土，心中就隐隐做疼。巨大的毁灭前的晕眩，你默默不语坐在我对面。你的泪水像突然打开的车灯，光束凄冷，恐慌，使我如同受到感召，闭上眼睛，僵立不动。我进入生存的恐惧，进入一无所有的状态。

　　爱过，你的照片竖在路边，下面埋葬着往昔无比美妙的事情。

　　一个人一生中被这么爱一次，足以摧毁他全部的余生。你的照片是一堵墙，墙外的那轮太阳；我被囚禁在一块全身能照射到阳光的土地上。

VIII

This photo you gave me: testimony.

Loved: buried by heavy yellow earth. My heart sprouts under your gaze; when you come toward me in June sky, it ripens, fruit flaunted on branches. Birds' fine talons scratching, rain and small rivers call, I dream in water.

Your picture intrudes. This orchard sags under fruit.

Loved: run down by love's semi. Again on land I move about, through swirling dust; dull pain still beats my heart. Dizzy before destruction, you across from me. Your tears like headlights snap on, beams, panic, my eyes roll back, possessed. In fear, enter existence, enter destruction.

Loved: your picture, signpost on the road; buried below, decaying beauty.

One person in one life loved this way one time, enough to destroy the remainder. Your picture is a wall; outside, sun. I am captive on a land shining to the sun.

九

那只在寂静中划过我的脸的手，如今在何处划动？现在我的周围一片寂静。

那枚在四周的孤独中掉在我心上的嘴唇，激起微小而久久不散的声音。那枚荧荧闪光的嘴唇，此时躺在哪里？也许边缘沾满泥土。现在我的生命是一段段的孤独。

现在我被记忆撕咬，独自行走在阳光柔和的田野上。野鸽子向我背后的天空飞去。往日注视我的眼波，那些沉默而颤动的眼波，此刻前前后后奔跑在我的腿旁，发出使我的心恐惧的叫声。现在我在田野上，孑然一身，向前行走。视野荒凉。

这是四月！我与你相识，过去得十分遥远的四月！

IX

That hand in silence crosses my face. Where to? Right now, surroundings, soundless.

Lips, in loneliness onto my heart. A tiny lingering voice. Lips, glimmering like starlight, rest where? Edges mud-stained? Now, lonesome distance.

Now I am torn by memory; I walk alone in soft, sunlit fields. Wild pigeons fly toward sky behind. Glancing into bygone days, speechless quivering glances, now darting back and forth beside my legs, noises that terrorize my heart. Now just me on the field, going. Field of desolate vision.

This is April! Our convergence, our gone April!

十

是的，那里就是我的故乡。我拖着两条蹒跚的腿，拄着诗歌的拐杖，脸上落满尘土，在你周围行走，寻找一条进入的路。那是一座心灵的寂静冷清的庄园，独自耸立，保持最初富丽的景象。

富丽，但寂寞，孤单。你的周围没有道路，一瞬间被丢弃的日子成为荒草，沿着你的城墙蔓延。那些歌，指尖的接触和流溢的湿润，在突然失去太阳的天空下迷茫，成为形状怪异的花朵，树和石头。炊烟升起，再也不飘回来。门被你的悲哀封住，永不打开。你的回忆是落满尘土的蛛网，密密麻麻，锁住每一扇窗子。那些窗子曾因往昔的幸福而辉映金色的阳光。这是寂静而孤零零的庄园，你给我爱情的地方。你去得非常遥远，它依旧冷酷地竖立在我的身上。

如今我面孔苍白，头发因岁月的消失变得斑斓。如今我唱那支怀念故土的歌。眼前到处是荒草，我寻找返回我心中的道路。周围一片寂静，只有毛皮斑驳的野兔从草稞里突然窜出，在我脚前跑过。那是一片荒凉里出现的"死"的意象。

是呀，那里就是我的故乡。是你给我爱的地方：那座我永远无法返回的家园。

X

"Where you love me,
there is the birthplace of my heart."

Yes, there, home. Dragging two staggering legs, leaning on this walking stick poetry, dust settling my face. All around you I search for entrance. One soul's desolate castle; aloft, alone, preserving.

Gorgeous, but lonesome. No inroads, all lost days wither edging your city wall. Songs, fingertips touching and moisture floating, perplexed under sun-forfeiting sky; now shapes of strange flowers, trees, rocks. Smoke from kitchen chimneys rises, does not float back. Doors sealed, by your sorrow, sealed. Your recollections, dust-settled spider webs, congesting each (once gold-reflected) window. Solitary manor, the place you loved me. You, away; it still erects, hardhearted, on my body.

These days, my ashen face, hair brightening as years disappear. These days I sing a longing song for native land. Before my eyes, everywhere barren. I search for paths to return to myself. From underbrush a mottled hare scurries across my feet. That, in desolation: death's calling card.

Yes, there, home. That place you loved me, that homeland where I can never return.

十一

现在又是四月！你看，干裸的枝杈上长出绿色的叶子，把一个个从中穿过的日子染得微微发绿。又是四月，这个充满魅力和谎言的季节！阳光吹着田野上的树干发出响声。你看那些走到户外的人，焦黄的脸因为感到晕眩而阵阵发红。四月，突然出现的明媚使我的四肢抽搐！

让我们走进四月，我的爱人！

在草地上唱那支歌吧；那支我们相识时，你站在阳光里唱的歌。我重新寻找那条细长的河流，幽暗，深密的果园；鸟的细细的爪印。唱那支歌吧，伸开四肢在你的歌声里躺下，在你心头缭绕的芬芳和细长的阴影遮住我的身体。

那支我会低声跟随的歌，我的爱人！

你的泪水，你的泪水使歌声变得秀丽。使我的心颤抖！

四月，残酷的季节！我们走到户外，在阳光涂深的草地上，注视那个日子从我们身旁跑过，那个我与你相识、相别的——日子！

XI

April again! Look, on brittle naked branches, green leaves, each day threading through branches, dyed newly green. April again, this coy season! Sunlight blows sound drying trees in the field. Look, people outside, sallow faces turning red. April, erupting; my four limbs twitch!

Shall we? Into April!

In fields, that song from meeting, from you in sunlight. I search anew for that long thin river, that shadowy orchard, birds' frail footprints. Sing, let me stretch open in your song, lie down in your fragrant refrain, filmy shadow cloaking my body.

My low voice, I trace your song, my love!

Your tears, the song. I shiver.

April, ruthless season! We, on sun-smeared earth, watching that day passing over us, that meeting and departing.

十二

你那封凄绝的信使我的心也变得凄绝。它在四月的花瓣中和野地里走着，流向心中的泪像脚底向前伸延的小路。我的心孤零零的。四周树木的枝干交叉缠绕，一些鸟儿凄厉地叫着，飞来飞去。

经过整整十二个季节！四月，许诺的时刻。也是这样，无数的花蕾怒放在我的周围，也是这样，我与你在一片荒漠里，没有声音的相撞，猝不及防。如今，我们在另一群枝头相遇。

我们互相摘采了。发育的部份各自保留。十二个季节轮流从稍头飞过，留下尖硬的干躁，留下围困在中心的水份。

我的心孤零零的！前方是被夕阳的光辉染成血红的天空。星星就要在远处出现了。当你强烈的刺疼远去时，悲怆的晕眩消失。我会在灯下读懂你全部的文字。

一些鸟儿凄厉地叫着，在我周围飞来飞去。

XII

Your sad, desperate letter; my heart also writes, desperate and sad. Through April's petal wilderness, toward me like the path before my feet. My heart, lonely. Tree branches intertwine. Birds, mournful and shrill, fly back and forth.

Twelve spans, we've completed! April, promised April. Buds blossom; you and I collide in a desert. This time, on another branch.

Plucked each other, ripe, keeping bitter parts for ourselves. Twelve times, taking turns taking off from tree tops, leave sharp-pointed dryness, leave moisture besieged at the center.

My heart, lonely! Blood-dyed sky, setting sun, then stars. Your pain, your nausea wink out. Below the lantern I digest all you write.

Birds calling mournful and shrill, all around me fly to and fro.

An Interview with Poet Xue Di

Releasing: Light and Darkness

By Edward Bok Lee

In 1991, two years after the Tiananmen Massacre, Xue Di wrote:

> "We now realize that, apart from vague, rebellious instincts, we know virtually nothing about ourselves. In an environment of free expression, we have lost our words. I stare at myself. I hear a new voice rising from my soul, the voice of my new self. I continue to write about what I know, about my confusion and pain, and about my awakening. I write about my efforts to learn a new culture in despair and ecstasy, about my thoughts on the gap between the two cultures...I write about my country which is deep in misery and crimes...about my love for the people who continue to fight for freedom and democracy..."

The following interview with Xue Di took place at Brown University in August, 1997 upon the poet's recent return from a visit to China for the first time in seven years. He came to Providence, RI, in 1990 as a writer-in-residence in the Freedom To Write Program at Brown University.

–Edward Bok Lee

EBL: You wrote criticism on fifty poems for a project on contemporary Chinese poetry that you also edited ["The Rolling Dice: Chinese Contemporary Avant-Garde Poetry—Dialogues"]. Can you talk a little about some of the non-Chinese influences on current avant-garde poets in China at this time?

XD: I think most Chinese avant-garde poets have been very influenced by contemporary European poets. Especially Baudelaire, Valery, and Rilke.

EBL: They're contemporary?

XD: Back to ten years ago, we believed these works to be contemporary, in some ways, avant-garde. You will find many Chinese writers who call themselves 'avant-garde' poets, but you will find a lot of romanticism in their writing. I think this is because of our strong poetic tradition. Classical poetry for thousands of years. Consciously or unconsciously, even if we want to cut off our connection with tradition, to do everything fresh, this long tradition carries over.

EBL: And how have more current avant-garde strains of American poetry, say Language poetry, influenced these writers, including yourself?

XD: There aren't many translations of Language poetry into Chinese. But when I was younger in China, I wrote many articles to introduce 'pure poems,' which might be something like Language poetry here. But I really believe that a good poem will be a good poem. If you have a deep meaning, a spirit, an internal life experience, in those words, among those words, behind those words…that will make the poem really great. But if you don't have more meaningful things behind the poem, the poem itself still could be beautiful if the words are carefully, beautifully, creatively arranged. There' s many ways to be a good poet. I don't reject Language poetry, but I am careful because when I was younger I was doing that a lot. Now I understand that for a poem to be good, language is not the only thing. It's not good enough if language is so pure, so beautifully and creatively arranged. There must be something else deeper and meaningful related to the human spirit.

EBL: You spoke at the University of Rhode Island last week about American ideology, capitalism. How do you see the American ideology of consumerism affecting Chinese literary production, in particular poetry, for which there's such a reverence for the past?

XD: That's one thing that's made this country [America] great. The desire to pursue new things. Constantly. In China, we value history and tradition and people will not so easily open their minds. It's risky to do new things. If you stay in the old way, you are already successful, so why break tradition? To be open minded, pursue new things, create new things, is not really the goal for the Chinese. How can you maintain the culture? That's the main thing.

EBL: After recently spending four months in China, do you see things changing?

XD: The door is wide open. But it's changing very slowly.

EBL: But then you've been living in the fast-paced United States for the past seven years. Do you feel living in the United States has liberated your poetry in any sense?

XD: I always felt that the inner lives of writers in China were free. If some people didn't dare write, that's their problem. When we talk about freedom to write, it's very interesting. Yes. The major reason I feel liberated is because I can see myself from so many different angles on a variety of levels. I was living in a closed society, now I'm living in a totally free society.

EBL: Has this affected experimentation in your poetry?

XD: I pay more attention to my internal experiences. It's abstract, but I feel it's more meaningful.

EBL: Can you be more specific?

XD: In my new poems, I have been trying to hold emotions, to push them back. To make the thing more dry, cool. Not emotional. Not reasonable at all. Calm, cool, to find something deep. To put things behind. Before I tried to put everything in front of the words. When I break a line now, it's natural that I break right there. The last word has rhythm, or power. It's hard to tell why I stop there. I don't want to add any more words. The next line starts totally differently. When I was young mostly it was linked. I had lots of emotions. Romantic. That's the big difference.

In the traditional way, also back to twenty years ago, my second line and third line could still relate to the first line.

Tradition was always following, without a real break. Now it's one line related to one thing, or reality. The next line quickly shifts to another reality. I use one line to describe this. The second line I try to not link to the first line, try to totally describe another view or thing. So those different views of the realities of subjects will create some impact between them.

T'ang dynasty poetry was so beautiful because lots were cut off, the form was extremely structured, limited, because they only had five words, so they had to choose different tones and words, they were forced to cut it off. For me, that was the beauty of T'ang classical poetry.

EBL: Post-modern.

XD: Yes.

EBL: Who are you reading now?

XD: I don't really read a lot in English yet. Some. I reread anthologies, Chinese, English, in translation. But mostly I've been reading myself.

EBL: In an interview with Arthur Sze, in "Mānoa," you referred to China as the root of your language. You write only in Chinese. What is your relationship to Chinese now in Providence, since you don't experience the language daily? Is the root drying up?

XD: I feel like the root is going deeper and deeper. There's definitely a lack of sensation of my culture, but I gain more sensation of my own spiritual life. So I cannot say which is better or worse for a poet.

EBL: I know you've become a jazz enthusiast.

XD: I love Duke Ellington, Louis Armstrong, Chet Baker, Thelonious Monk, Stan Guess, John Coltrane — one of my favorites, Billie Holiday, and Miles Davis, definitely. When I was in China, I didn't know jazz at all.

EBL: Can you talk a little about how jazz has influenced your writing, if at all?

XD: The rhythm, the style, is full of life's desire and pain and joy and depression, and life's struggle. There's so much behind it. I feel it's also not direct. Classical music tends to go out. I still enjoy classical music, but I don't like dramatic things too much now. I like when the emotion is hidden, really pressed inward.

EBL: Does this influence the rhythms of your own poetry?

XD: Probably, potentially, under. If everything affects my life, it will come out in my poems. I try to transfer some jazz into my poetry, I'm not trying very, very hard, but I've been conscious of this. I've never researched the rhythms of jazz. I feel like whatever I absorb, my poems will bring out. I don't know how or what, or where.

EBL: What changes do you see in your poetry? What ways have American culture and ideology and life in Providence (New England) influenced your poetry if at all?

XD: Mostly it's because I have more options here. Life was limited in China. Internally I could be free and broad in China, but society was lacking information. I was lacking in connections. Here in New England I try to reach my life in many different ways. I don't try to use another style to write a poem, I never think about it. The style changes because my life is changing and developing. A new form and style comes out to suit my new thinking and feeling (of living here).

I feel like I'm living deeper. I'm not living on the surface: I'm happy, I'm not happy, I'm going against society, I'm not going against society. Mostly, I have so many options here. Whatever I want to do, I can. When I was in China, there was no challenge, you only have one thing to do, but here you have so many options.

EBL: Do you ever feel isolated here in Providence?

XD: I'm ready to be lonely because I understand being lonely, solitude, this really helps me to focus on my internal life.

EBL: Isolated physically, but also linguistically. Has speaking English daily affected the rhythms or imagery of your poetry?

XD: I don't think speaking English affects my rhythm because when I'm writing I'm writing in Chinese. But potentially, very subtly, something's influencing it, but I'm not conscious of this. One thing I can tell you in my consciousness is the way to... [pause] ...when I was in China, I wrote very big. I released my emotions toward the whole of society. In America, people and society are very detailed.

The way people talk is very detailed. Even the structure of English is very detailed. You have to say I'm happy, of what? I'm angry, of what, with what, about what? Americans ask. In Chinese you just say I'm angry. I think this is a cultural difference.

EBL: Between East and West.

XD: Chinese pursue, focus on completion more than details. Western society is so scientific, so you have to focus on details. Without details, there's no whole. In China, the whole thing is first, then come details.

EBL: And this has affected your poetry.

XD: Yes, I'm really focused on details more now. Line by line, word by word. This was not conscious before. I went back to China last year. I went to a poetry conference where people discussed my new poetry. This is a very contemporary, avant-garde style," they said. "So many details, the images, the views." When I looked at the poetry, I said "Yes." I really had a lot of details. In China, no one really writes that way. Because it's still about emotion. Everything comes out. But for me I have the general idea, but the meaning is not singular, it is scattered. Each meaning has its own individual meaning. Only when you put all the individual meanings together, can you see the complete meaningfulness. That's one aspect of a postmodern sensibility. The Chinese asked, "How many collections of contemporary American have you read?" "None," I said. They accused me of lying. Of writing in a postmodern style. I told them probably because I'm living in that society, I'm absorbing all the styles and ways people focus on the details. So I am forced to tell details. Clarity. I've been trained in this style. Because my life is more detailed, the poem comes out more detailed.

EBL: Is this possibly an example of American culture having touched your subconscious?

XD: Yes. But this is about style. Details are also related to life's feeling. The new poems I've been writing are about living in a society full of choices, options. I feel like I'm able to get into myself. I'm confirmed. I want to be a poet, a writer, a good writer. I want to plant my feet into the soil, like roots, going deeper and deeper, being conscious, aware, patient with whatever I'm doing.
There's also lots of comparison with my past, culture, serious thinking about my life, self-understanding, self-retrospection. This really made my poetry become more and more different. In terms of the content, the meaning. It's not just about style.

EBL: Content influencing form.

XD: I'd like to emphasize that I think content is mostly from one's spirit, which is what poetry is about.

EBL: Because Russia and China came to consumerism later than other nations, it's easier to see how they're being affected. Do you feel the ideology of American-style capitalism is more or less conducive to poetry than Chinese-style communism?

XD: I think [American-style capitalism] can mix well with

poetry. Everything can mix well with poetry, because poetry is the experience of life. If people experience that kind of lifestyle, live that way, it will definitely match the poetry. Coca-Cola and entertainment and enjoyment of life are another thing. I'm not extreme and go against development of more enjoyment and consumption to feel and enjoy life more, but when you sink too far into it, people begin to lose the sensation of the spirit. Because the more you encourage your body to encounter the consumption, all the consumption, the less relation you have to the spirit.

EBL: Why is that necessarily so?

XD: If you live a quiet life, you can understand yourself. Capitalism can be very noisy: bars, rock-n-roll, concerts, beach, vacations.

EBL: And jazz concerts?

XD: That's different. Rock-n-roll for me is releasing, bringing everything out, screaming out your emotions, feeling of life. When you release that much you can become inhuman. You see all the violence at rock concerts. You don't see this kind of violence with jazz. Emotion is dangerous when it's flying around, hanging in the air. Emotion doesn't go deep. Emotion gives you power to release a lot of things, but it doesn't help you seriously think about your life. That's the way I wrote poetry while living in China. Emotion can make an artist very powerful, very strong, but how deep? You could say emotions are one of the deepest things in human life, but I feel how much really dark...[pause]...you're not just showing dark, you also have to put lights inside the dark, to light the darkness, to let people see the shape of darkness, to let them see in the center or behind the darkness that there is a light. That's the whole point, in my understanding. I feel rock-n-roll is sheer darkness; releasing all the emotions. There's no release of light. There's nothing really going down into the ground. I don't mean I don't like rock-n-roll. I like the Doors, but jazz and new age and classical and opera have touched me more. You have to feel something going up and coming down. Then you feel complete. You don't feel cut off, like you're flying around in the wind with pure emotion. You have to have something that really stays with your soul. Stay with the depths of human life. That kind of understanding and feeling probably makes you a good writer, a good artist. Without those things, I doubt it. You could be good at one specific thing, a very good Language poet, and very good emotional poet, but that's very narrow. I'm talking about writing as a way to understand life, a way to express one's feelings related to that life.

EBL: How is this releasing of emotion different in poetry for you?

XD: I'm releasing, but that's one end: going up. In the meantime, another end is reaching down. It's like a tree. I always feel that my life should be like a tree. The topside is going up to the sky, to receive sunshine, but the roots are going down down down. The deeper the roots are, the higher the tree can rise.

采访诗人雪迪

光与黑暗

采访者：爱德华·鲍克·李

爱德华：您曾经撰著了一本研究中国当代诗歌的书，其中有您评论五十首诗歌的文章〔《骰子滚动：中国大陆当代诗歌分析与批评》〕。请您简单谈谈目前中国先锋诗人受到的一些外来影响。

雪迪：我认为大多数中国先锋诗人都在很大程度上受到当代欧洲诗人的影响，尤其是波特莱尔、瓦雷里和里尔克。

爱德华：那是当代的吗？

雪迪：10年前，我们认为这些作品是当代的，在一定程度上也是先锋的。你会发现许多中国作家自称是"先锋"诗人，但他们的作品带有浓重的浪漫主义色彩。我想这是因为我们有悠久的诗歌传统的缘故。古典诗歌有几千年的历史。即使我们想切断与传统的联系，尝试全新的东西，这个悠久的传统还是会在有意无意间承继下来。

爱德华：美国诗歌中那些更新的先锋流派，譬如语言诗，是如何影响这些作家的，包括您本人在内？

雪迪：语言诗译入中文的并不多。几年前我在中国的时候，倒是写过许多文章介绍纯诗。所谓"纯诗"，有点象这里的语言诗。我认为，一首好诗就是一首好诗；只要字里行间表达深刻的意义，一种精神，内在的经验，就可能成为一首好诗。假使诗中没有深刻的内容，但字、词安排、联合得准确、新颖，仍可以成为一首优美、耐读的诗。我不排斥语言诗，但持谨慎的态度；早些年我写了很多这样的诗。如今我懂得，一首诗要好，语言不是唯一的因素。一首诗，光语言纯，用词炼句地道，有新意，还不够上乘。诗歌必须含蓄深刻的内容，诗歌必须映现人的精神。

爱德华：您上周在罗德岛大学的讲演中谈到美国的意识形态和资本主义，请问您如何看待美国的消费意识对中国文学产生的影响，尤其是诗歌，曾经是那样的被崇敬？

雪迪：这是让美国这个国家伟大的地方，有永远追求新事物的欲望。在中国，我们重视历史和传统，人们不轻易表达自己的思想，做新的事情也有风险。如果你停留在习惯中，你已经获益了，干吗还要打破传统？保持心胸开阔，追求和创造新事物，不是国人的目标。怎样保持已有的文化和平稳地置身于习惯，这才是重要的。

爱德华：最近您在中国呆了四个月，有没有看到什么变化？

雪迪：门敞开了，变化依旧缓慢。

爱德华：过去七年您一直生活在快节奏的美国。您是否觉得，生活在美国在某种意义上解放了您的诗歌？

雪迪：我感到被解放是由于现在我能从许多不同的角度审察事物，在不同的层面上关照文化、社会和自我。我曾经生活在一个封闭的社会，现在我生活在完全自由的国家，这二个极端赐予的冲击力和创造力是巨大的。

爱德华：这是否影响了您在诗歌创作方面的实验？

雪迪：相对于诗歌写作技艺，我更注重内心世界的经验过程。我以为这更有意义。

爱德华：您能否谈得更具体些？

雪迪：在新作里，我努力控制情绪，不使情绪爆发；不渲染，保持冷静；不动感情，也不理性化；镇定，冷静，发掘深刻的意义；尽量含而不露。以前我用言词把一切都表达出来；如今我尽量不表达，只是表述、呈现，然后强烈的表达会自己从行与行的空隙间、词与词的连接处涌现。如今我断行，自然地就断在那儿。末尾的词携带节奏和力量。我说不清为什么停在那里，为什么经过这里；就是不要再多走一程，多加一个词；而下一行与刚开始的又无关系。过去我写诗大多是相联的。实际上那样的相连带来更多阅读上的阻碍和断裂。现在我写得断和跳跃，但却提供了阅读的和谐、使读者的想象力展开的可能。想象力是艺术的本质，如同大地上的水，人的心脏。思想是光。

按传统的写法，或是在二十年前（那时我充满感情，浪漫），我的第二行和第三行仍与第一行关联。传统的写法是行行相联，中间没有跳跃。现在是一行描述一个事物，或一个现实；下一行马上转向另一个现实。我用一行描写这个事物；下一行不与上一行相联；下一行是焕然一新的景象，是新事物。这些不同现实的景象在转换之间创造了力量，使美具有形体。

唐诗所以如此美，是因为许多东西被砍掉了。格律诗结构严谨，限制性强。由于一行五言七言，古诗人必须讲平仄，字斟句酌。他们必须砍掉可有可无的东西。对我来说，这就是唐诗美的地方。

爱德华：后现代的。

雪迪：对。

爱德华：你目前在阅读谁？

雪迪：我还没有开始用英文阅读。我读翻译成中文的诗集、诗选；更多的，我审视自己。

爱德华：施家彰（美国新墨西哥州桂冠诗人）曾经采访过您，采访文章发表在"Manoa"上。在那次采访中，您说您语言的根在中国，您只用中文写作。如今您生活在新英格兰的普罗维登斯市，并不天天接触母语。您现在与中文是一种什么样的关系？您的根是不是正在干枯？

雪迪：我觉得这条根掘进得越来越深了。
是的，在日常生活中，对于母体文化的直接感受减少，但感觉力和观察力却更敏感、更尖锐；对词和汉字更敏感，更有体验和灵动，更有创造性；最重要的，是对自己精神生活的感受和追求更强，从而使诗包容更多层次。孤身一人在异国他乡，这也许就是一个创造者能尽力而为的了。

爱德华：我知道你是爵士乐的爱好者。

雪迪：我喜欢杜克·艾灵顿，路易斯·阿姆斯特朗，切特·贝克，薛乐尼额斯·曼克，约翰·柯特伦，这是我极喜欢的爵士乐手，还有碧丽·苕利德，当然还有迈尔斯·戴维斯。我在中国的时候，没有听到过爵士乐。

爱德华：你能谈谈爵士乐是如何影响你的写作吗？

雪迪：爵士乐的韵律、节奏，这样的风格，曲调中充满对生命的渴望。你感受得到那些痛楚，欢乐，孤独，挣扎，这一切隐蔽在旋律后面，会在任意的一个瞬间爆发，令你震惊和感动！它们不是直接的到来的。古典音乐趋向于直接的打动你。我仍旧喜爱古典音乐，但现在不是太喜欢戏剧性的事物。我喜欢情感隐藏，力量朝向内心。

爱德华：这是否影响了你的诗歌的节奏？

雪迪：有可能，是潜在的，默不作声的影响吧。如果这些那些影响了我的生活，就会有新的内容和写法出现在我的诗中。我尝试把爵士乐移入我的诗歌，不是很卖力的尝试，而且这也很难，但我意识到我在努力。我未曾深入研习爵士乐的韵律和节奏。无论我感受、吸收到什么，我的诗歌都会呈现，无论何时何地，新的意识和感悟都会在我的诗歌中出现。

爱德华：您在自己的诗歌中看到什么样的变化？美国的文化和意识形态以及您在普罗维登斯市的生活都在哪些方面对您的诗歌产生了影响？

雪迪：在这里我有更多的选择，在中国会受到限制。在中国我的内心世界可以是自由和开阔的，但（那时的）社会缺乏信息。我不具有和外界的联系。在这里，在新英格兰，我努力在多个方面拓展我的生活。我不强用另一种风格写诗，我不忧虑此点。风格变了，是由于我的生活在变化和发展。新的写作风格的出现，是为了适应、应合我的新思想和丰富的感受。

我生活得更深刻。我不是生活在表层：我幸福，或者不幸福；我反对什么，或者不反对什么。我在这里有许多选择，想做什么都可以。我在中国的时候，生活缺乏挑战性和多样化，我只可以做一件事。在这里我有选择，可以行动。

爱德华：您在普罗维登斯市可有被隔绝的感觉？

雪迪：我做好准备孤独。我将在孤独、寂寞中，把注意力凝聚在内心生活上。

爱德华：不仅人隔绝，语言也隔绝。每天讲英语有没有影响到您诗歌的节奏和意象？

雪迪：我不认为讲英语影响我的节奏，因为我写作时用的是中文。当然也可能会有某种微妙的影响，不过我还没有意识到。有一点我意识到了，可以告诉你，那就是…［停顿］…在中国的时候，我写得很大。我向整个社会抒发感情。在美国，人们的生活和制度运作都充满细节；人们谈话的方式也很细节化；甚至英文的结构也非常细节化。你必须说因为什么而觉得怎么样。我说我愤怒，美国人就问：因为什么愤怒？对什么愤怒？在中文里，我说我愤怒就完了。我认为这是文化差异。

爱德华：东西方之间的差异。

雪迪：中国人（东方人）追求、关注的是完整，而不是细节。西方社会十分讲究科学，所以你们注重细节。没有细节，当然也没有了整体。在中国（东方），整体是第一位的，然后才是细节。

爱德华：而这影响了您的诗歌。

雪迪：我现在十分注重细节。写作时，我逐字逐行地关注。这以前没有。去年我回中国时，在北京参加了一个诗歌研讨会。会上，诗人、评论家们研讨了我的新作。"这是非常现代、非常先锋的风格"，他们说。"这么多景象、意象、细节"。我自己一看，也说："是啊"。我真的提供了许多细节。在中国诗人们不这么写，他们仍然在抒情，一切都表达无遗。我的诗虽然有个主题，但意义不是单一的，而是分散的；各个意义独立存在。你只有把这些分散、独立的意义联合起来，才能领会深厚的总的涵义。这也是后现代意识。诗人和评论家们问我，"你读了多少本当代美国诗集"？我说，"一本也没读"。他们说我撒谎，认为如果我没读过后现代的西方诗，怎么会具有后现代的写作风格。我告诉他们，也许是因为我就生活在那个社会，吸收了人们注重细节的习性。我不经心地把细节说了出来。说清楚，这是日复一日我在生活中受到的训练，也是我在美国的社会上感受到的行为指南。由于我的生活更细节化，我的诗歌创作也显得细节化。

爱德华：这也许是美国文化已经浸入到了您的潜意识之中？

雪迪：是的。但这是关于风格。细节联接着生活的感觉。我写的这些新诗是关于生活在一个充满选择和机遇的社会里的感受。我觉得我能够进入自我了。我下定决心，做一个诗人，做一个优秀的作家。我要把双脚伸入泥土，象根一样，越扎越深；有意识地、清醒地、耐心地做我正在做的事情。

与过去相比，许多方面发生变化；对文化及生活的严肃思考，对自己的理解和生命的回顾，等等。这使我的诗歌与先前的越来越不同。我是说在内容和意义上，而不仅仅是风格的变化。

爱德华：内容影响形式。

雪迪：我认为内容主要来自人的精神，而诗歌是关于人的精神的。

爱德华：俄罗斯和中国的消费意识比其他的国家要晚，因此比较容易看到影响的过程。你觉得美国资本主义的意识形态比中国的共产主义更有利于诗歌吗？

雪迪：我认为美国的资本主义能够很好的与诗歌结合。任何事物和意识形态都能与诗歌结合，因为诗歌是人生的经验。人们体验那样的生活方式，在其中生活，其中的精髓必定会与诗歌相遇，在诗中展

现。可口可乐、娱乐、享受则是另一码事。我并不
极端反对生活里的享受与消费，但当你沉溺的太
深，跟随的太远时，你会失掉与精神的连接，你对
精神的感悟会萎缩。你越是鼓励你的生命消费，这
样那样的消费，你与精神的联系就越稀少。

爱德华：为什么一定这样呢？

雪迪：如果你过着宁静的生活，你可以领悟自己。
消费和享受的过程会很吵闹：酒吧、摇滚、音乐
节、海滩、加上度假。

爱德华：那么爵士音乐会呢？

雪迪：这是不同的。对于我摇滚乐是释放，是把所
有的情绪全放出来，无保留。情感发出尖叫，生命
伴随发泄。当你那么无遮无拦的释放，你有可能变
得危险。我们在摇滚音乐会上看到那些暴力，但你
不会在爵士音乐会上看到暴力。情绪是危险的，它
们飞来飞去，把在它们前面的东西撞碎。情绪不往
下沉。情感，充满力量的释放，不帮你细致地思考
你的生活。这是我在中国的写作方式。情感能使艺
术家很有力，很强大，但会有多深？你可以说情感
在人类生活中是很深厚的，但我看到那么宽阔的黑
暗…[停顿]…你不是仅仅表述黑，展现黑，你要在黑
暗里放上一盏灯。你把黑暗点亮，让人们看见黑暗
的形状，让人们在黑暗的中心或者黑暗的后面看见
亮光，看到光明。这就是我要说的，这就是我的理
解。我认为摇滚乐呈现的是激情，是激情后面的黑
暗。它释放了所有的情感，这些情感里没有光，没
有可以凿破地表进入深层的力。我不是说我根本就
不喜欢摇滚乐。我喜欢乐队"门""皇后乐队"等，但爵

士乐、歌剧、古典音乐和新时代音乐更打动我。你
要感觉到气流向下也在向上，然后你体验到完整。
你没有感到只是被骤然切开，你在风中旋转，被情
感裹带着。你要知道你有着能和你的的灵魂呆在一
起的东西，它能够驻扎在人类生命的深处。这样的
理解和感觉有可能使你成为一个好作家，好艺术
家。没有这样的意识和认知，我不知你能走多远。
你可以很擅长做一件事，一个地道的语言诗人，一
个情感充沛的诗人，但你走过的还是一道窄门。我
是在说写作是融入生活的开始，是带领我们向上并
且逐渐抵达高处的过程。
爱德华：情感的释放在你诗中又是怎样的呢？

雪迪：我会解放，情感的顶部向上；在同时，还有
一股下沉的力，这就好比一棵树。我想我的生活应
该是一棵树：顶端要插入空中，吸入阳光，但根向
下挺进。树根越深，树愈高大。

Xue Di:
June Snow, Falling Elsewhere

An Interview for Brown University's "Year of China"

Interviewer: Alexandria Sheng

During the 2011–2012 academic year, Brown University hosted a series of public lectures, cultural events, academic conferences, and exhibitions aimed at undertaking a comprehensive exploration of China. Titled the "Year of China," this initiative delved deeply into the rich cultural, economic, and political landscape of the Greater China region—tracing its history, examining its present, and looking toward its future. This interview was conducted in May 2012, during the course of this year-long program.

AS: So I just wanted to start off by thanking you for participating in the Year of China Oral History Project . . . From a personal standpoint, I just want to say that reading through the articles and different interviews that have been conducted, it was really refreshing for me to hear your personal take on what it was like to grow up in China during the Cultural Revolution . . . because, as someone who is Chinese, and as someone who has lived in Asia for the majority of my life, and in Beijing for the past five years, I feel like it's a part of my own background that has been silenced because many of my relatives and other people who have undergone that process are not willing to talk about it. So, I just wanted to ask you what it was like to grow up in

China during the Cultural Revolution, and what your early life was like before you came to the States?

XD: First of all, I would like to thank you for arranging this interview. And to answer your question I have to start from . . . I was born in 1957. I was born and grew up in Beijing. When I was six years old, my parents divorced.

At that time, the percentage of divorces was very low in China, because the working unit, the governors, and the government tried very hard to control peoples' divorces. So they do not, even if people are not living or getting along well, they still do not permit peoples' divorce because at that time, everything needed paper or permission from the working unit or government for whatever kind of thing.

So the reason they did not allow people to get divorced was because then they could show Western society that China has a better societal system . . . that everybody is living really well, they get along, they have a happy family, you know, we are very happy with our own life, with the living style. So back then, when I was six years old and at school, the children did not really understand why . . . they never encountered anything like that so they thought I was the reason for my parents' divorce. So I was bad, a bad one.

At the end of school each day, I had to run very fast because the children wanted to beat me, they wanted to punish me, and I did not understand. I went home and asked my father why this happened, and my father could not tell me anything. At that time, I was living alone as a young child because my mother remarried, my father remarried, and my stepmother actually did not accept my living with them, so I had to live in a dormitory. Every night I went through nightmares — afraid of silence, afraid of quietness, afraid of footsteps in the hallway. I had to put things against the door to secure myself. So that was my life at night. And then during the day, I had to go to school and endure that humiliation and fear.

And then the 1966 Cultural Revolution happened in China and lasted ten years until 1976. During this period, all the schools, colleges, and universities were shut down, and we had no school. That was the time I was supposed to go to college but I could not go because there were no universities or colleges that were open. The intellectuals, professors, and teachers were sent to the countryside to live with peasants to have their minds "re-educated." The Cultural Revolution was against any foreign literature or contemporary art; the ideal for the Cultural Revolution was a return to tradition and back to the common way. Of course, there were other reasons, political reasons, but apparently that was the phenomenon. That was the kind of environment I was in growing up.

For my personal life, it was very confusing and painful; societally, there was turbulence, violence and the closing down of good education. At that time I was very good at science. My teachers wanted me to develop this interest, but my parents were doctors and wanted me to study medicine. With the kind of life I went through, however, and with what was going on in society, I just did not want to pursue this.

One day, I found a collection of poems written by Alexander Pushkin, the Russian poet. The book had been abandoned in a hallway because back then anyone who owned a book like that would be in big trouble. So I read that collection of poems, and for the first time I felt so much love, there's so much sunshine, there's nature, there's all kinds of beautiful things inside that book and in those poems, so far away from the daily life I'd been living. So that's how I became interested in literature and started to become a poet.

AS: Yeah, I was actually very interested to discover that, in one of the interviews, you mentioned that the first person who inspired you to write poetry and who opened your eyes to the beauty of poetry was Alexander Pushkin, and then the second one was Charles Baudelaire, and then the third one was William Yeats. And I was very interested to discover that your primary literary influences were all Western authors, because I think Chinese literature — like Tang poetry — is something that is very ingrained in the culture and is something that all children grow up knowing and reciting, and is something that is very central to the culture. So my question is, first of all, how did you find something in these poets that was outside of . . . like, during the Cultural Revolution, all this material was banned. How did you get access to it? And did you read it as a translation?

XD: Yes, I was reading these works in translation. Don't forget, at that time, during the Cultural Revolution, we basically cut off the connection between ourselves and our tradition, classical poetry. And that's one reason, I mean, again, back then, there's no education, no teachers, no leaders to educate us, to teach us how to follow tradition;

there was no such thing during the Cultural Revolution. So that was one reason I — and my entire generation — did not read or focus on our own tradition and classical poetry.

And also, our big fantasy back then was to try to read as many works of world literature as we could get our hands on, because we lived in such a closed society, and we didn't have a good way to get information. Our minds and thoughts were controlled by society, by the party. So you can imagine that, living under these kinds of circumstances, how much we want to open ourselves to receive things from the world. That's one of the reasons why we were trying our best to find the treasure, the literature, from the world to read. Of course, at that time, most of the works we could find were in translation. Reason one was that we had cut off the connection with our tradition because of the Cultural Revolution and reason two was that we were so eager, so thirsty, so hungry for the fruits of Western society.

But now, to live in the United States, to live in a foreign land, and to think about my original culture again, I feel like I'm paying so much more attention to classical poetry, the Tang dynasty, Sung dynasty, and all the treasures and beautiful things of writing. All of my new writing still contains my contemporary thinking, situation, expression, and experience, but for the writing skill and technique, I'm paying much more attention to our classical poetry. I really absorb and draw so much from classical literature.

AS: You said the Cultural Revolution ran from 1966 to 1976 and then you came to the United States in 1990. What was your life like in that period? One of the articles mentioned that you were organizing writers and poets into support groups to support the Tiananmen demonstrations. Can you tell me a little bit more about that?

XD: Sure. As I mentioned earlier, there were no universities or colleges in operation, so when I graduated from high school I went to a specialized two-year training school. Don't forget, back then, when people graduated, most of the students had to go to the countryside, just like during certain periods in this country you had to serve in the military at a certain age. Back in China during the Cultural Revolution there was no choice. When you graduated, you had to go to the countryside to have your life "re-educated" with the local people, with that kind of lifestyle.

Since my parents were divorced, I lived with my father. He and his second wife did not have other children, so I was the only child for that family. Back then, certain kinds of exceptions were granted for not going to the countryside. One reason was if you were a single child in a family with aging parents, you could remain home to look after them. Since I was in that situation, I was very lucky and did not have to leave Beijing and go to the countryside. But during high school we still spent months and months training with the army, and I did that, but I did not have to spend three to five years of my life during the Cultural Revolution to go to the countryside, fortunately.

So instead I went to a special training school to learn how to make light bulbs. At that time, they cut the staff of the institute, but they still needed people to work for them. The whole system was messed up and there was no school that could send kids directly into these factories or institutes, so they had to create a kind of special training school to provide another way for new members to work there. So I attended this school and had two years of training, and then I worked in the film lighting institute, to make light bulbs, to project the film and evaluate the quality. In cinema, when you project film, it uses a very high beam, and the light bulb usually has a very short life. So one aspect of the research involved trying to extend the light bulb hours. I worked there for 8 years. Of course, I did not particularly like this kind of work at that time and started to put more energy into my writing.

In China, if you work in a factory and get an illness, you can stay home and still get a fairly high percentage of your salary, like say 80%, as a form of social welfare. That's one thing that China was always so proud of—they would say that they really treated their workers well. So I thought I would try to take advantage of that, and I learned from a friend how to fake an illness so I could get sick leave as a way to stay home and do my own writing. And it worked. And that's how much of my writing in China was produced during those years.

Also, that's why during the Tiananmen Square demonstration in 1989, I was able to go to the square and participate. I was a member of the Beijing Writers Association and I wanted to do something to support the students to pursue freedom of writing, freedom of expression. I was able to do this independently and not be caught right after the movement crashed down, since I was not working in the unit and could not be tracked or accounted for by the authorities. I was on my own as an individual, and they did not have any actual proof at that time that I actively participated in any activities.

In the meantime, in 1990 I received the Hellman/Hammett Award from the Human Rights Watch in New York. My life in China was increasingly in danger because they were trying to collect evidence of my involvement with the student democracy movement. Brown University through the novelist Bob Coover had established the Freedom to Write Program within the Creative Writing Program that year in response to the Tiananmen Square massacre and to help writers from around the world in dire circumstances. They issued me an invitation for a writing fellowship along with two other Chinese writers. That's how I was able to come to the United States in January 1990.

AS: So my understanding of the Brown Freedom to Write Program was that it was offering a chance for Chinese dissident writers to leave the country and come to the States. How did they discover your poetry?

XD: Back then, in 1989, I already had a translation of my work available in this country. Also, my translator had passed on my work to PEN America. And in 1990, I received the Hellman/Hammett Award, sponsored by the Fund for Free Expression, an affiliate of the Human Rights Watch in New York. Since PEN America already knew my work, they contacted several different universities in the United States such as Harvard, Yale, Princeton, all the top universities, and Brown was among them. The novelist Bob Coover and President Vartan Gregorian worked together to establish a program to help Chinese writers and they established the

Freedom to Write Program.

We came to Brown, two poets and one novelist; the novelist came from Paris and another poet was already living in New York City. I was still in China and was invited to come to the United States to participate in this program. I had a really tough time trying to get a visa to leave China because I had a tough time getting a passport. In China, usually back then, nobody had a passport, they just had identification to prove where they lived. To leave the country we had to first get a passport, and then get a visa.

For my situation, I had less trouble getting a visa, but more of a problem getting a passport. (For people who have a less literary background, they have less trouble getting a passport but more trouble getting a visa.) So I spent three months waiting for a passport, and that's a whole long other story . . . I went through a very difficult time when they were trying to prove that I participated in the Tiananmen Square student movement, but they did not have any actual evidence.

So finally, after three months, I received my passport. I received my visa two weeks after that since the American Embassy was already familiar with my case. They did not actually think I would be able to get a passport. So as soon as I got my passport I went to the American Embassy, and they said, "Yes, we already know your case, so we will just issue you a visa quickly." That's how I finally got my visa to leave China and come to this country.

AS: You said that when you were writing poetry in China, a lot of what you communicated was sort of an outward energy, like fighting the system, fighting your childhood, fighting the constructs of society, and that that was where you gained your value. So when you came to the States and there was nothing to fight against, you felt lost and started to look inward. So do you think that the development of your poetry has sort of accompanied your journey through that transition, from sort of concentrating your energy on the outside to looking more into yourself in an introspective sense?

XD: Absolutely. You know, poetry definitely closely reflects peoples' own history. Poetry is an expression of understanding toward your life, and the emotion towards objects, and the relationship between yourself and your outer and inner worlds. So in a different stage, you have a different kind of understanding and lifestyle. Poetry and any works of art always reflect that. So while I was in China, as I said, because we live in such a closed society, all we want to do is see more of the outside world — freedom. It's like we live in a room with no doors, no windows, no lights. All you want to do, all you can do, is chisel, fight with the wall, chisel again, try to create a little bit of a hole, a crack, to see the sunlight, to hear the birds sing, to see some kind of green color. So all the energy, actions, these are all fighting something, something really close to you, something that oppresses you, something that makes you afraid, with all the fear surrounding you.

So I will say, for my writing style back then in China, it was more outwardly directed, with lots of emotion, lots of shouting and anger; you just want to get it out. And when I came to this country, such a free country — of course there are a lot of reasons why you might not feel free, such as being under family or other kinds of burdens, but in general, I'm talking about freedom in mind, in thinking, in that sense it is a free country. So free, so many options. I felt the fighting energy all of a sudden disappear, because there is no object, no opponent in front of you. You don't have to fight society, because society provides so many possibilities for you. I started to feel that there's nothing for me to fight against. I then understood that to grow up in a communist country, all we learn is to fight, to survive, to complain, to feel unfortunate about our lives, with very little time to think about our inner world or our interior experience very deeply as a human being. In these circumstances, what kind of depth could be reached? What kind of internal experience could you really access? Because there was no such environment in China to foster this.

When I came to Brown University, I was well-funded at that time for the first few years, which gave me time to think about my life, my lifestyle, my culture. I started to gradually turn inward, to direct my energy, thinking, and emotion toward the inside, to go deep within myself, to think more as a human being . . . the thinking, the way of thinking, the way of life, and what I could do. So I put more energy into my own being, and my writing naturally evolved in a different direction. In China, there was a lot more emotion, but since I came to this country my writing has become deeper and quieter, with more energy directed toward the inside. I feel connected with the depth of being, of living. This is much more profound than the way I lived in China.

AS: And you mentioned that poets must speak from a vantage point that is elevated, almost disengaged, from society, and that poets must speak not just from their individual psyche but from a sort of collective consciousness that transcends both space and time. So how does someone go about achieving this perspective and how do you think your own experiences have enabled you to look through that global lens?

XD: There are many writing styles that connect, that relate to, the way of peoples' living. So for me, since I had a really tough childhood, living in a chaotic and unfair, even cruel, society that violates human rights. Since I went through that, I'm not just thinking of myself and writing poetry to cry about my own miserable life and my pain, anger and fear. I'm thinking more through myself as a solid being to understand the living world, to understand society and humanity. So that's my way of living, my way of writing.

The deeper I understand myself, the deeper I understand humanity. Then, the more I could devote myself to humanity, to society, through poetry, through writing and criticism. That was my choice for the way of living, not just to cry for myself, but also to cry for the injustice in our living world, and the poverty and violence and all the kinds of things that are in danger of making our world unhealthy, making people suffer. So I would like to, through my poetry, my writing, like to talk to, speak to, all the kinds of people affected by these things. Or, to put it another way: if it's all joy, it's not just my joy, it will be the joy of all the people.

AS: Do you think, in that sense, poets sort of have a sense of duty to communicate what, perhaps, people who are suppressed or people who don't have that voice, to communicate a global sense of emotion and injustice, and how do you think poetry achieves that in a way that prose doesn't?

XD: Poetry and prose are two different kinds of forms. Poetry is tighter, and there is more imagination within it; you leave a lot of space for people to feel. And in prose you can say everything you want to say, you tell people one, two, three, four, five, six, until ten. But for poetry, the difference is if there are ten things, you only tell three or four. You leave those five or six as empty spots, empty spaces, for people to bring their life into it, then to stimulate their own life perception and imagination to participate with you. That's the difference between poetry and prose, one difference between poetry and prose.

But to answer your question: for me, living in a foreign country now, I don't have the fear of being punished or persecuted if I'm saying something or writing something honest, I don't have that fear. So of course I have more duty or obligation to tell more, to follow my heart, to not feel fear of writing, much more than people who still live in that kind of circumstance. I believe that poets and all good artists should not just work with their own craft to make it "prettier," although that's one thing they may feel they need to do; the main thing is to really get into your own world to understand our living world better. I believe that is what the path is supposed to be.

When a person has creative talent, this is not only for the artist's own daily life. I believe the gift of the artist, when they're really following their own heart, their heart should feel other hearts as well. The heart of the artist should not only contain or feel its own pain, or desperation, or joy, it should also receive and connect with the pain and joy of humanity. This gift of the artist should also really receive that part, feel that part, and present that part, too, through its own skill, own style of art. That's what I believe. Not everyone thinks this way, a lot of people just think that art is pure art. More broadly, if a person is in touch with himself, in touch with his own heart, through that heart, one should feel more things behind, surrounding, and beyond.

AS: So you write your poetry in Chinese, and last month at the John Nicholas Brown Center on the panel with Amitav Ghosh, Ha Jin, and David McKirdy, you mentioned that now, as your English starts to improve, you started to fight with your translators about how they translate particular words or terms in your work. What are some of the difficulties or the frustrations you've faced in translating Chinese to English? As in Chinese, each word is sort of a prism that refracts a lot of different meanings and has cultural connotations, and means so much more than just the word in itself. So, do you feel like that sense of culture, or cultural understanding, is lost when you translate?

XD: I believe that from one language to another, each language has its own culture, its own meaning, and its own depth. A lot of things are so particular to it, so that only this one language can really describe what is happening. Unfortunately, poetry is not like painting or music, where you do not need a translation. For painting, music, or sculpture, these things are between your eyes and your heart, you already have a connection with it. But for writing, for people to understand, you have to translate from a language. So from one language to another language, the essence of the language's soul, more or less, will be lost.

When you write a Chinese word, it has its own picture, you can see the picture. For example, my name is *Xue Di*. The first name *Xue* means snow, so when you write "snow" in Chinese, you almost feel like snow is falling on the ground through this character. So when you translate that, of course, that aspect will be missing. Each language has its own pace, rhythm, sharpness, and the history of that will all more or less be lost. But in terms of the meaning of the language presented, I don't think this will be too endangered. The thinking, the consideration, can carry from one language to another. But the uniqueness of that language is going to be missing.

However, really good translators can actually build the history or the beauty of a language and translate this into and make good sense in another language. They can carry over all the meaning, all the thinking, the expression of a thought from one language to another. I believe this part can be carried over. So, unfortunately, there's no other way to do it, it has to be done this way — if the translator is able — to build up a lot of beauty and meaning in the translated language, so that this will still be achieved.

That's why translations of poetry remain in place for years and years; they will never vanish, and people always appreciate them, like when I read Alexander Pushkin, or Baudelaire, or W. B. Yeats. I fell deeply in love with those poems, even though I was reading them in Chinese. Of course, if I read those poems in English they will present a totally different kind of beauty. But since the translation was so good, I felt complete beauty in the translated language, and it touched my heart and it touched generation after generation in China.

AS: I just discovered that *Xue Di* is actually your pen name. So can you talk about why you chose that particular name to represent you or your poetry?

XD: My original name is *Bing Li*, or *Li Bing*. *Bing* is the first name, *Li* is the last name, the family name. *Bing* is one of the most popular given names in China. In Chinese, there could be many meanings of *Bing*. *Bing* could be "soldier," *Bing* could be "ice," or *Bing* could be "polite." During the Cultural Revolution, a little red guard, or soldier, was one of the most popular images in China, and lots of parents chose *Bing* as the first name for their children.

Li is the largest family name; although China has thousands of family names. We had many emperors in history whose last name is *Li*. They would reward people who were loyal to them by saying, "I will give you my family name," which meant that those people would have the family name *Li*, then pass this on generation by generation. That's why *Li* is a very popular family name in China. *Bing Li* put together is one of the most common names in China, like in this country, "John Smith." For a poet to have a very popular name was not actually good, however.

I remember a time when a friend of mine knocked on my door (we did not have telephones back then) to say, "Hey, you just published a really bad poem—how could you even dare to publish it?" And I said "What are you talking about?" So he showed me the newspaper and I saw that it was exactly my name, *Li Bing*! But, he was right — the poem really was bad! This kind of thing happened several times. If I was walking on the street and heard someone call out *Bing Li* I would stop, turn around, and see another nine or ten guys turning around as well. So I finally decided to give myself a unique name that nobody else would have and only represent myself.

Growing up in Beijing, the capital city with such a huge population, you could barely see nature, no trees, no green color — the environment was not even considered a deal back then during the Cultural Revolution. Although I went through really painful growth during the Cultural Revolution, I loved nature, but did not have much of a chance to be in nature while I was living in Beijing. The only chance I had to see nature, to feel beautiful nature, was when snow fell and the ground was all covered with pure white snow, that was one of my happiest times as a child.

I remember one time when I went to the park, I was sliding with just my boots on a big snowy hill and opened my arms and I felt so free, I thought I could fly. Then I fell over and got ten stitches — as you can see, I got into a lot of those kinds of accidents. Since I loved snow so much, I thought I would give myself a name associated with it. My pen name is *Xue Di*. The first name "*Xue*" means snow, that gave me a comfortable feeling of being in nature; that's the only time I could feel pure and touched, and not worry about how dirty the world is, at least in my life back then. "*Di*" means revelation.

Chinese has four tones. For example, *ma* can be spoken in four different ways: mā, má, mǎ, mà. They're all spelled as *ma* in Pinyin, but the four tones have four totally different meanings. *Mā* could be mother, *má* could be numb, *mǎ* means horse; *mà* could be abuse. You have to be careful with the pronunciation and tones.

Back to the pen name, "*xue*" is actually the third tone, a softer tone, and you want to make the next tone sharper, so I added "*di*" as in revelation. I like the look of the "*di*" character, it looks solid. "*Xue*" looks pretty, "*Di*" looks solid to get it in balance. Also, the sound . . . one is a little bit of a swallowing sound, another is spoken out clearly. So that's how I created my name, *Xue Di*.

Back in China this was the only name of its kind, because nobody, no family was named *Xue*, and no family was named *Di*, so I thought it was really great. But now, if I look at the websites and type in "Xue Di" in Chinese, I will see — I don't know what happened — the name *Xue Di* is so popular! *Xue Di* is the name of a beer company, a shoe company, a hotel in Milan, a tavern, a clothing house, a sock company, even an underwear company. If I knew how popular my chosen name would eventually become and had registered it , I would be really rich! Of course, there was no such registration back then.

But it's very clear to me that my name has been essentially stolen, because that's a name that could only come from a creative mind and from a compelling reason to put "xue" and "di" together. So fortunately or unfortunately, the name has spread out. They obviously found my name from my publications in China and then registered their businesses. I got nothing from it.

AS: So you went back to China in 1997. Have you gone back since?

XD: I went back to China in 1997 because I had come to this country in 1990 and seven years had passed. In those seven years, I did not dare to go back to China, because back then it was still post the 1989 democracy movement. I was still afraid to be caught or persecuted if I went back. So I waited until 1997. That was the first time I went back to China and I was lucky to get in. I stayed in my father's house, but my father's phone was tapped. Although I was followed, I did not, at that time, participate in any serious literary events, so I was able to return without incident.

And since 1997 I have returned to China four times; a couple of times I went to different places; Tibet, for example, and Hong Kong for the International Poetry Festival. The other times I went back just to visit my parents and travel in China. The last time I went back to China was five years ago. Now I work full-time in Media Technical Services at Brown but can only take two weeks off at a time. This is too brief for me to go back to China. Every year my parents ask me, when are you coming back? I say, I don't know, we'll see. So that's the situation.

AS: So what's your relationship to China and to your parents right now? How do you view them…what are your feelings toward them?

XD: I still talk to my parents every week. I call my mom every Monday night, mostly because I love to play table tennis, I go to the League, the Rhode Island Table Tennis Club, to play in the league every Monday and Wednesday to practice. This is in addition to my writing, my work at Brown, and my tutoring business in Chinese. So when I finish playing on league night, that's usually when I have a little bit of time to talk to my mom. There is a 12-hour time difference so 12 to 1 o'clock at night here, when I'm finished, is their noon time or afternoon time. So I am able to communicate, talk to my parents, by phone. They are not in good health because they are getting old and did not get a lot of exercise like in this country, which is a way to protect their health. So anyway, I am able to talk to them, but not see them face-to-face or go back to visit them, but still, luckily I can talk to them. Also, I have a younger sister who lives in New York. She used to do painting and sculpture, and now she takes care of her daughter. During the Christmas season and around Independence Day I will go to New York to spend a week with her and her family.

AS: So what are your feelings toward China? Do you have a hatred for the past, the history that it has gone through?

XD: Whatever happened to me in China, that's just my life. I don't hold anything from my childhood, my personal misery. For the country, of course, there is forever agony and shame that's crying toward humanity. If you ask my feelings toward China now, I have a lot of anger and grief and feel desperate for my country. While the economic situation is improving, people's living circumstances, the environment for free thinking and expression, are getting worse and worse. People are oppressed and persecuted harshly, and still do not have freedom of speech, freedom of expression. If people post something online, they could get in serious trouble. Things are actually almost worse than 1989. There is so much crime and violation of the Chinese people.

Even people who have lived in a certain place for generations are told: we need to take your place because we need to build buildings or because we need to make some kind of business in this area, like an amusement park, then those people will be forced to leave their own homes. And they get very, very little pay, maybe not even 30 percent of the value of their house. Say with $15,000, they would only get four or five thousand dollars. There's so much violation of their rights, forcing them to move.

And so the reason I'm talking about this is just to tell you that it's not only about thinking, consideration, freedom of living free, it's even just your own right to live in your own home, even that is violated. And so to see what's happening in China, I feel heartbroken, I feel very, very angry and sad. The only thing I can do is maintain communication with friends of mine who live in China and express these feelings through poetry.

AS: So how does ping pong fit into all of this?

XD: When my parents divorced, I was so young, I had to try so many different things to see what would save me from a miserable life. I imagined I could be a sailor, an officer, or whatever you can imagine. Ping pong, back then and now, is a very popular sport in China, actually it's the second largest sport in the world. China is the strongest country in table tennis right now, and back then it was very popular.

My father wanted me to see if I could be an athlete, so I had two years of formal training playing table tennis, four hours every day of basic strokes, competition, and analysis of style, that kind of thing. That's how I started to play ping pong. But after two years of this kind of training, I felt like I did not want to live my life this way. The feeling of pain and confusion kept growing inside my body, my mind, so to play table tennis did not really help at that point. I knew I had to do something else to really find the answer of why I'm living this way, why my country is going through this.

As I mentioned, at 12 years old, I found a collection of poems and started to find another path. I wanted to write, I wanted to become a poet. I found that after writing, I could have some peace of mind. To be a poet made me feel the meaning and pride of life. I then stopped playing ping pong and lived essentially as a poet. After I came to this country in 1990 and stayed a couple of years, though, I had a chance to get reacquainted with this sport. I made some friends who also played table tennis. They said, that's a good sport; I said, I know it's a good sport. They asked if I knew how to play. I said, a little bit. My friends mentioned a local table tennis club and said don't worry, we'll teach you. So I said okay.

I went to the club with my friends and beat them badly! They had no idea. I thought it was good exercise, table tennis is a really good sport, not just physically for the body. You have to use your legs, your arms, you have to do complex footwork and weave in and out. It's also a quick sport—the ball can cross the table at 120 mph and you only have a few seconds to react to this speed. When world class players spin the ball, that's like 9000 revolutions per minute. So you can imagine what it would take to handle that kind of power and how much effort and flexibility the sport requires. Table tennis is a great sport . . . not violent, very physical, very strategic. Some people say table tennis is just like chess.

I think that I've been living my life in my own world — of course, I go out and connect with the outer world, but all the energy is inner, always quiet and solitary in feeling. Table tennis provides a good opportunity for me to be with people, to release emotion, to see wins or losses right away.

To write a good poem, even though you think it's good, to see if it really is or not takes time, takes a lot of criticism, and peoples' reading. But in table tennis you get results right away. I kind of like that, so for that reason I still play. For ten consecutive years I was State League champion, I was really involved with the sport and still am.

AS: Okay, last question. So what's your favorite poem that you've written?

Xue Di reads poem:

Hotel Viking
Translated by Hil Anderson and Keith Waldrop

In the wake of a prefabricated passenger ship
the ocean, as if with an old cotton blanket

weighs deeply on a body wide awake
The sky in the eyes of a scattered school of fish

grows brighter and brighter. The bridge that spans the
brine crosses also the opaque middle-aged mind

dark path between two precise terms
My mother grieving

writes to her faraway son
Waterbirds, lonely, follow the lights

toward regions of cold where they hover
This evening the hotel room's thermosystem

thundered without rest. Number 634
said the key in the unlit hallway

In my homeland some valuable
persons are disappearing

雪迪：六月的雪，飘落在它处

布朗大学中国年访谈

采访者： 亚历山德丽娅·盛

怀昭（译）

在2011至2012学年期间，布朗大学举办了一系列公开讲座、文化活动、学术会议及展览，旨在对中国进行全方位的探索。这项名为"中国年"的活动深入探究了大中华地区丰富的文化、经济与政治面貌——既回溯其历史，审视其现状，亦展望其未来。本次访谈正是在2012年5月、即该活动举办期间进行的。

Q：感谢你参与中国年口述历史计划…读过你的文字和各种访谈之后，我很想听听你自己的故事，听听在"文革"时期的中国长大是怎样的一种经历。我想问的是，在"文革"期间长大是什么样，在来美国之前你早期的生活是什么样的？

雪迪：感谢你安排这次采访。要回答你的问题，我必须从…从我出生讲起吧。我1957年出生在北京，在北京长大。我六岁那年，父母离异。当时，中国的离婚率是非常低的，因为工作单位、领导干部、政府都想方设法控制这类事情。即使夫妻生活相处得不好，他们仍然不容易分开，因为凡事都得工作单位或政府批准、盖章才办得到。他们不会轻易批准离婚的，因为他们需要向西方显示，中国有更好的社会制度…每个人都生活得很好，他们和谐相处，家庭幸福。所以，当我六岁那年，在学校里，孩子们得知我父母离婚了的时候，他们真的不明白为什么…因为从来没有遇到过这样的事。他们就以为是我的原因，我父母离婚肯定是因为我不好，因为我是个坏孩子。

每天一放学我就快跑，因为我不想挨打，我不明白为什么别的孩子要打我。我回家问爸爸，为什么会这样，可爸爸也说不出什么。那时候，我是个孤单的孩子，因为母亲改嫁，父亲再婚，我的继母实际上不能接受我和他们一起住，所以我不得不一个人住在宿舍。每天夜里我都会做噩梦，怕静，怕走廊里的脚步声。我会用东西顶在门上，让自己感觉踏实些。晚上的生活就是这样。到了白天，我不得不去上学，忍受屈辱和恐惧。

然后就到了1966年，文革开始了，持续了整整十年，一直到1976年。

在此期间，所有的学校，学院啊大学啊都被关闭了，我们都不上学了。这时到了我该去上大学的时候，却没有大学可上。知识分子，大学教授，老师们都被赶到乡下，跟农民一起生活，接受他们的"再教育"，改造自己的思想。外国文学、当代艺术，所有这一切都成为文革的批判对象。文革是中国大陆的一场灾难，我们称之为十年浩劫。我就是在那样一种环境中长大的。从我个人经验上来说，那是一种非常迷惘和痛苦的经历；在社会层面，国家经历了动荡、打砸抢的暴力和教育上的缺失。那时我在理科方面表现比较出色。我的老师希望我能发展这一兴趣，而我的父母都是医生，希望我学医。可我的生活经历，加上当时的社会气氛，使我不想往这方面发展。于是有一天，我读到了一本俄罗斯诗人普希金写的诗集。这本书是被人遗弃在走廊里的，因为那时候，拥有这样一本书会给自己惹来麻烦。我读了这本诗集，第一次感受到这么多的爱，这么多的阳光，感受到自然，所有这些美好的事物都在那本书里面，存在于那些诗行之间，带我远离了我生活的那个世界。所以，文学成了我的兴趣所在，我开始成为一个诗人。

Q：是啊，我其实很感兴趣地发现，有一次在采访中，你提到普希金是启发你写诗，和打开你的眼睛看到诗歌之美的第一人，然后第二个是波德莱尔，第三个是叶芝。我感兴趣的是，你最初受到的主要文学影响都来自西方作家，而不是中国文学——像唐诗什么的，我以为那种影响应该是根深蒂固的，是所有中国孩子成长中都知道和背诵的东西，是文化中非常核心的部分。所以我的问题是：首先，你是怎么发现到这些外来的… 比如，文革期间被禁止的作品。你是如何接触到的？你读到的都是翻译过来的吗？

雪迪：是的，我读到的是中译本。不要忘了，在文革期间，我们的传统是被割断了的，这也包括我们与古典诗词之间的联系。这是一方面原因——我的意思是，那时没有学校可上，没有老师来教，没有人引导我们如何遵循传统；文革时期没有这样的事情可言——所以我，我们整整一代人，没有能够专注于自己的传统。同时，作为禁书，世界文学对我们充满了诱惑，一旦能辗转拿到自己手上，我们读起来就如饥似渴。毕竟，生活在这样一个封闭的社会，获取外部资讯都成了一种奢侈。我们的头脑和思想都是由社会、党控制着。可以想见，在这种情况下，我们多么希望向世界敞开自己，去接纳更多的事物。这就是为什么我们尽可能向外部探求，努力寻找知识宝藏，从文学中吸取养分。当然，我们能找到的是翻译成中文的作品。所以，一方面是文革割断了我们与传统文化的联系，另一方面是我们对西方文化如饥似渴。但现在，住在美国，生活在异乡，当我重新思考我的文化之根，我发觉自己醉心于唐宋诗词之美，对中国古典文学越来越重视。我新的写作仍充满我对当代情境的思考，从表达到经验，但在写作技巧上，我更多地吸收和借鉴古典文学和诗歌传统。

Q：你提到文革是从1966年到1976年，而你来到美国在1990年，当时又是什么样的一个时期？有文章提到，你当时正组织作家和诗人声援天安门的示威。

雪迪：对。正如我前面提到的，当时没有大学可上，所以我高中毕业后去上了两年的培训学校。别忘了，当时学生们都上山下乡去了，有点像适龄的人必须服兵役一样。文革期间又没有别的选择，毕业了就得去到农村与村民同吃同住，接受他们的"再教育"，接受那种生活方式。由于我父母离异，我跟我父亲生活，他和他的第二任妻子没有孩子，所以我算是家里的独子。按照当时的规定，有些特殊情况下是可以豁免上山下乡的。其中就包括如果父母年迈，家里又只有一个孩子，那么你可以留下照顾他们。我就是属于这类情况，所以我很幸运，没有离开北京到农村去。虽说高中时还是去军训了好几个月，但所幸没有被迫去乡下耗费三、五年的生命，而是去了一个特殊的培训学校，学习制造灯泡。那时候，教育和研究机构虽然都不存在了，但工作仍然需要有人来做。整个分配系统乱套了，没有受过教育的人就直接进入就业阶段，所以一种特殊的培训学校就应运而生，其目的是职业训练。我就是进了这样一所学校。在进行了两年的培训后，我就进了北京电光源研究所，制造胶片投影灯泡和从事质量鉴定方面的工作。电影院里面的投影是使用强光打上去，灯泡的寿命通常很短。因此，我们研究工作的一个方面就涉及如何延长灯泡的使用寿命。我在那里工作了8年。当然，我不太喜欢这样的工作，所以开始将大量精力投入写作。我就想办法托病，用休病假的方式呆在家里写啊写。我在中国的写作大部分都是在这期间完成的。也因此，在1989年天安门广场示威期间，我能够比较投入地参与这场运动。我当时是北京作家协会会员，我就想做些什么来支持学生对言论自由的追求。我之所以能有独立的空间去做这件事，而且在"六四"遭到镇压之后没有立即被抓起来，就是因为我一直以病休的借口不去上班，所以没能被当局跟踪上或施加什么压力。我等于一个人单干，他们没有能有效收集到我参与任何政治活动的实际证据。在此期间1989年9月，我收到设在纽约的人权观察颁发的赫尔曼/哈米特奖。这时我在中国的处境变得越来越危险，因为他们开始收集我参与"六四"民运的证据。那一年，作为对"六四"大屠杀的回应，也为了帮助世界各地处境艰难的自由作家，小说家鲍勃·库弗（Bob Coover）通过布朗大学设立了一个"自由写作计划"。他们给我及另外两位中国作家发出了写作奖学金的邀请。就这样，我在1990年1月来到美国。

Q：据我理解，布朗大学是要通过这个自由写作项目，为中国的异议作家提供出境的机会。他们是怎样发现你的诗作的？

雪迪：当时，我在1989年已经有作品在美国翻译出版，我的译者还将我的作品转给了美国笔会。1990年，我获得了由纽约人权观察赞助的赫尔曼/哈米特奖。由于 PEN 美国已经对我有所了解，所以他们联系了几所美国的的大学，如哈佛，耶鲁，普林斯顿等顶尖的大学，布朗大学也在其中。小说家鲍勃·库弗与该校的校长Vartan Gregorian 一起，促成了这样一个项目，为中国作家提供支持的自由写作计划。我们来到了布朗，两个诗人，一个小说家；小说家是从巴黎来的，另一位诗人已经在纽约生活。我呢还在中国，拿着赴美的邀请函。我为了取得赴美的签证而费了不小的周折，因为我想办法先拿到一本护照。那时候在中国，一般人是没办过护照的，从小到大有的只是一个户口本，作为户籍证明。要想出国首先必须拿到护照，然后才能去办签证。以我的情况来说，我获得签证不是什么难事，但拿到护照却不那么容易（按理说应该是办护照比较容易，办签证比较说不准）。所以我为了办护照就足足等了三个月的时间——这过程够写一部长篇小说的。我那段时间过得非常煎熬，因为当局想习难我，想抓我参与天安门学生运动的把柄，但又找不到任何实质性的证据。所以最后，三个月后，我终于拿到了我的护照。两个星期后，我的签证就批下来了，因为美国使馆已经对我的情况很熟悉了。他们实际上并没有想到我能拿到护照。因此，我一拿到护照就去了美国大使馆，他们一见到我说，"是的，我们知道你的情况，我们会很快发给你签证。"这样，我离开了中国，来到美国。

Q：你提到过，当初你在中国写诗，多是传达一种向外的能量，与体制对抗，与自己的童年对抗，与社会的结构对抗，在此过程中你有了自己的价值。那么，来到美国，那些要对抗的东西瞬间从你眼前消失，你感到失落，并开始向内审视。所以，你的诗歌创作是否也伴随了你的这一心路旅程？

雪迪：绝对如此。你知道，诗歌肯定反映着诗人自己的历史。诗歌是对你所理解的生活的一种表达，折射着你对事物的情感，以及你的外部与内部世界之间的关系。因此，在不同的阶段，你有不同的理解和不同的生活方式。诗歌，以及任何艺术作品，总是会反映出这一点。所以，我在中国的时候，正如我所说的，由于我们生活在这样一个封闭的社会，我们总是尽可能地向外部伸展，想要看到外面的世界——渴望自由。这就像我们生活在一个没有门，没有窗，没有灯光的房子里，所有你想做的事，你所能做的，就是凿墙，凿啊凿，跟这堵墙较劲，努力地凿个洞出来，或者哪怕只是打开一个裂缝，为了得到一点阳光，听到鸟儿唱歌，看到外面的绿色。因此，所有的能量，行动，都形成一种对抗，针对那些压迫你的东西，那些包围着你的恐惧。所以我会说，我在中国时的写作风格是外向型的，带有很多情绪，很多呼喊和愤怒；一心想把它释放出来。当我来到这个国家，这样一个自由的国度——当然你也可能在很多方面仍然并不自由，比如要面对家庭或其它各种负担，但在一般情况下，我是指思想自由，在这个意义上它是一个自由的国家，给你这么多自由，这么多选择，令我感到对抗的能量突然间消失了，因为没有了对象，在你面前没有了对手。你没必要跟这个社会较劲，因为这个社会已经为你提供了这么多的可能性。我开始有一种失落的感觉。后来我明白，成长在一个共产主义国家，我们学到的所有东西就是对抗，艰难图存，一旦觉得不幸就会抱怨，往往无暇顾及内心世界和思考一个人内心深处的经验。当我来到布朗大学，最初几年我得到很好的资助，这给了我时间去思考我的人生，我的生活方式和我的文化。我逐渐转向内省，把我的能量、思想和情感导向内在，向内深入挖掘，去更多地思考作为人的命题… 思想，思维方式，生活方式，我能做什么。所以我的写作也自然地发生了方向性的变化。在中国时，我在写作中注入的更多是情感，但自从我来到这个国家，我的写作变得更深沉，更安静，更多向内的能量。我觉得自己开始与更深层的存在相联系。这比我在中国时的写作要深刻得多。

Q：你还提到，诗人必须站在前卫的、甚至不从属于这个社会的立足点发声，诗人不能只是表达他们个体的心绪，而是要从某种超越时间和空间的集体意识出发。你是如何从自己的经验来透视这个世界的？

雪迪：写作风格往往是与人的生活方式有关的。对于我来说，由于我有一段苦涩的童年，曾生活在一个混乱的、不公正甚至残酷的社会里，感受到人权所遭受的侵犯，所以我不只是想着自己和通过写诗来发泄我自己的悲苦，愤怒和恐惧。我想的更多的是通过自己这样一个具体的存在，去了解世界和人性。这就是我的生活方式，我的写作方式。愈深入了解自己，也就愈深入地了解人性，也就愈能够通过写作将自己投身到人类和社会中去。这是我选择的生活的方式，不只是为自己呐喊，而且还针对我们生活于其中的世界上所有不公、贫困和暴力，以及各种各样带给人类危险和痛苦的东西。通过我的诗，我的写作，为所有受这些东西困扰的人们诉说。或者，换句话说：如果一切都充满喜悦，那不只是我一个的喜悦，那将是所有人的喜悦。

Q：那么，从这个意义上说，在全球意识下的沟通诉求和情感表达上，你是否认为有什么是诗歌能够达到而散文所达不到的？

雪迪：诗歌和散文是两种不同形式的写作。诗歌更严谨，且有更多的想象空间，里面有很大的留白供人们去感觉。而在散文中，你可以言无不尽，你可以一五一十。诗歌不同，诗歌是要说出一半，留下一半的空白给你回味，给你代入自己的生命，来激发你自己的感悟与想象。这是诗歌与散文的区别。但是，对你提的这个问题，我要说的是：对我来说，生活在异乡，不用为所思所想担惊受怕，不用因为诚实的写作而恐惧，我当然有更多的责任和义务，要替那生活在另一种环境的人们诉说和写作。我相信，诗人以及所有优秀的艺术家都不应该只是把自己的活儿做得"漂亮"，虽然这也是需要做的；更主要的是要真正进入自己的世界，更好地了解身处的世界。我相信这才是该走的路。当一个人具备创作才华的时候，这就不仅是针对艺术家本人的日常生活而言。我相信艺术家的天份在于，当他们真正听从内心的时候，他们的心也应该感受到他人的心。艺术家的心里装的不应只有自己的喜怒哀乐，它会与人类的悲欢紧密相连。艺术家的天份使得他能够通过自己的技巧和风格，去接纳、感受并呈现出他与人类相连的那部分。我相信，并不是每个人都这样认为，很多人觉得艺术就是纯粹的艺术。如果你在更宽、更深的领域来讨论艺术，那就是一个人与自己的联系，对自己内心的感受，并通过内心去感受事情背后的，周围的，或超越的东西。

Q：你是用中文写诗的。上个月在约翰·尼古拉斯·布朗中心 (John Nichol Q Brown Center)，你与阿米塔夫·戈什 (Amitav Ghosh)、哈金、David McKirdy 出席研讨会时，你提到现在，随着你的英语有了进步，你开始与译者为你诗作中一些特定字眼的翻译发生争执。在将中文翻译成英文的过程中，你到底经历了怎样的困难和挫折？在中文里，每个字都像多棱镜一样折射着很多不同的含义，其文化内涵往往超出一个字的字面意思本身。那么，在翻译过程中你是否觉得会丢失某种文化上的感觉？

雪迪：我认为，从一种语言到另一种语言，每种语言都有自己的文化，其本身的含义，和自己的深度。有很多东西在语言方面是如此独特，只有这一种语言能够真正描述它发生了什么。不幸的是，诗歌不像绘画、雕塑或音乐那样，这些东西无需翻译，直接存在于你的眼睛和你的心灵之间，与你直接沟通。但对于写作来说，为了让人看懂，你必须先翻译，而从一种语言到另一种语言，这过程中或多或少地，会有些语言的神韵流失掉。当你写出一个汉字，它是象形的，你首先看到的是图像。例如，我的名字叫雪迪。当写出第一个字"雪"的时候，几乎可以感觉像雪飘落在地面上一样。当你翻译的时候，当然，这种感觉将会丢失。每种语言都有自己的速度，节奏，尖锐性，这些在翻译中都将或多或少地失去。但从意思本身上来说，我倒是相信翻译的问题不大，因为思维、思考是可以从一种语言转换成另一种语言来表达的。但语言的独特性将被丢失。然而，真正好的译者是可以在一个语言的历史基础上，将语言之美尽可能地转移到另一个语言中去。他们可以尽可能承载所有的语义，所有的思维，思想，用一种语言表达另一种语言。我相信，这部分是可以承转的。但无论如何，不幸的是，除了翻译成另一种语言，有没有其它办法可以让写作实现跨文化的了解。这就是为什么诗歌翻译一直存在着；译作将永远不会消失，就像我到处读到的普希金，或波德莱尔，或者威廉·巴特勒·叶芝。我深深地爱上了这些诗，尽管我是通过中文来阅读它们。当然，如果我用英语读这些诗，它们会呈现出完全不同的另一种美。但由于翻译得非常好，我完全沉浸在它们译成的文字中，它们打动了我，也在中国打动了一代又一代人。

Q：我才发现，原来"雪迪"其实是你的笔名。那你可否说说你为什么会用这个笔名写诗？

雪迪：我原名李冰。无论是我的名还是姓，在中国都是最流行和最有代表性的。李是中国百家姓中最大的家族姓氏之一。中国历史上有许多皇帝姓李。还会赐姓给效忠者，然后代代相传。这就是为什么李姓在中国是一个非常大的姓氏。"李冰"放在一起更是中国最常见的名字之一，就像在美国起名叫"约翰·史密斯"，对于一个诗人，有一个非常流行的名字本来就不是很好。我记得有一次，一个朋友来敲我的门（我们那时候电话还不普及），说："嘿，刚刚看到你有一首诗发表了，写得非常糟糕，怎么竟然敢发表呢？"我问："你在说什么？"于是我看到报纸上，跟我同名同姓，李冰！而且，他说对了，这首诗确实写得非常糟糕！这种事情发生过几次。有时我走在街上，听到有人喊一声"李冰"，我会停下来，一转身，看到还有其他十个八个家伙也转身。所以，我最终还是用笔名，起一个独一无二只代表我的名字。我在北京长大，在这个人口庞大的首都，几乎看不到大自然，没有太多树和绿意——文革期间人们根本不把环境当回事。虽然我在文革期间的成长经历真的很痛苦，但我热爱自然。然而在北京生活的那段时间，我并没有多少机会置身于大自然当中。仅有的欣赏大自然的机会是下雪的时候，大地铺上皑皑白雪，这就是我最幸福的童年时光之一了。我记得有一次去公园，我穿着普通的靴子从大雪覆盖的山坡上滑下来，我张开了双臂，我感觉到自由，感觉自己快要飞起来一样。接着我就摔倒了，为此头上缝了十针——正如你看到的。类似的磕磕碰碰那时还有不少。由于我热爱雪，所以我给自己起的笔名第一个名字是"雪"，它给我一种在大自然中的那种舒适的感觉；它让我为一种纯真而感动，而不被世界肮脏的一面所困扰，至少在我当时的生活中是这样。"迪"指的是"启迪"。汉字有四声，像"ma"的四声，有四种完全不同的含义。妈　mā　【阴平】，可以指母亲，　麻　má　【阳平】可能是麻木了，马 mǎ【上声】就是马，骂 mà【去声】可就要小心了（还有吗 ma【轻声】），你必须小心发音要准。回到笔名，"雪"是第三声【上声】，一个柔和的声调，那么我会想让下一字的发音高扬起来，所以我用了第二声【阳平】的"迪"字。"雪"字漂亮，"迪"看起来结实而有平衡感。另外，从发音上，"雪"有一点含音，而　"迪"则是清晰地吐出来的。我就这样给自己起了雪迪这个名字。那时在中国，雪迪还真是独一无二的名字，因为百家姓里没有姓雪的，所以我认为这真是太棒了。但现在，如果上网键入"雪迪"二字，就会看到——不知道怎么回事——雪迪这个名字已经很普通了！　它现在成了一个啤酒的牌子，还有一家鞋业公司也叫雪迪，米兰有个同名旅馆，小酒馆，甚至制造袜子和内衣的企业，等等。早知道我的名字这么受欢迎，我当初应该把它注册一下，这样我就发财了！当然，当年也没有注册商标这回事。但是，对我来说这很清楚，我的名字基本上是被盗了，因为这名字只可能来自于创意思维，并且要有一个令人信服的理由才会把"雪"和"迪"两个字结合起来。所以，幸或不幸，这个名字已经广为流传。他们显然是从当年我在中国的出版物中发现了这个名字，然后注册了自己的企业。我却从中一无所获。

Q：你在1997年回了一次中国，后来呢？

雪迪：1997年，我回到中国，在我去国七年之后。在那七年里，我一直不敢回到中国去，因为当时中国仍处在1989年"六四"民运的后遗症中，我还是害怕回去后被抓或遭迫害，所以我一直等到1997年才动身。那是我1990年离开之后第一次回到中国，我很幸运还能入境。我住在我父亲家，但我父亲的电话被窃听了。虽然我被跟踪，但我当时没有参加任何严肃的文学活动，所以还能够平安无事返回美国。自1997年以来我已经四次回到中国；我去了不同的地方：例如西藏，还有香港的国际诗歌节，也去看望我的父母，顺道在中国旅行。我最近一次回到中国是在五年前。现在我在布朗大学媒体技术服务部做全职工作，一次只能请两个星期的假，这么短的时间回中国是太仓促了。每年我的父母都问我，你什么时候回来？我说，我不知道，等等吧。就是这种情况。

Q：那你现在与中国及你父母的关系如何？你如何看待他们..你对他们的感情如何？

雪迪：我每周会跟父母通话。我每周一晚上打电话给我母亲，主要是因为我喜欢打乒乓球，我打联赛，每周一和周三去罗德岛乒乓球俱乐部练球。这是我在写作和在布朗工作之余的另一个生活内容。所以，当我打完联赛的晚上，通常我会有点时间跟我妈妈聊聊。这中间有 12 小时的时差，所以我这里晚上 12 至 1 点钟，是他们的中午或下午时间。我通个电话跟父母交谈一下。他们身体都不太好，因为上了年纪了，又不太运动。但无论如何，所幸我们还能通话交流，虽然难得相见。另外，我有一个妹妹住在纽约，她以前搞绘画和雕塑，而现在在家照顾女儿。每逢圣诞节和美国独立日，我会去纽约与她和她的家人共度一个星期。

Q: 那么，你对中国的感受又是如何呢？你对它所经历的过去还怀有仇恨吗？

雪迪：无论我在中国的时候经历了什么，那都是我的生活。我从不讳言我的童年、我个人经历过的痛苦。至于这个国家，它所经历的苦难和耻辱永远在向人类诉说。如果你问我对现在的中国怀有什么样的感情，我有很多的愤怒和悲伤，我为我的国家感到绝望。虽然经济状况正在改善，但人民的生活环境，在言论自由和思想表达方面，情况是越来越糟糕了。人们仍受到打压和严厉迫害，如果人们在网上传播自由的思想，他们可以会给自己惹来麻烦。这方面情况几乎比1989年时候更糟。中国人民的权利受到如此严重的侵犯，政府仍然可以随时以发展的名义推倒你的祖屋，为了建一个游乐园而将原住民赶出自己的家园。我说这些的原因就是要告诉你，不仅是人的思想自由受控制，连你住在自己家里的自由也可以被侵犯。所以，看看中国的现状，我感到心碎，感到愤怒和悲伤。我能做的就是通过诗歌把这种内心情感表达出来。

Q: 那么，借此机会，读一首你的诗让我们感受和回味吧。

威金人旅馆

沿着成批客轮驶离的方向，
海水像用旧的棉被

沉沉地压在缺觉者身上。
天空在散开的鱼群眼睛里

越来越亮。那座跨过盐水的桥
也跨过中年人大脑里的黑暗。

路途的黑暗，在二个精确的词之间。
独身的母亲悲哀时

就给远行的儿子写信。
孤独的水鸟沿着灯火

向更冷的地域飞翔。这个
夜晚，旅馆房间的调温器

不停止地轰鸣。号码 634，
当我拿出钥匙，黑暗中

一些最优秀的人
正在我的祖国消逝。

关于作者

　　雪迪出生于北京。他是四卷中文诗集和一本当代中国诗歌评论集的作者。他的英文译作包括五部完整诗集和四本小册子。他的作品在众多美国文学期刊和选本中发表，并被译成多种语言。雪迪曾两次获得赫尔曼／哈米特奖，获得布朗大学的茹科夫斯基奖学金，并获得兰南基金会奖学金。

About the Author

Xue Di was born in Beijing. He is the author of four volumes of collected works and one book of criticism on contemporary Chinese poetry in Chinese. In English translation, he has published five full length books and four chapbooks. His work has appeared in numerous American journals and anthologies and has been translated into several languages. Xue Di is a two-time recipient of the Hellman/Hammett Award, a recipient of the Artemis A. Joukowsky fellowship through Brown University, and a recipient of the Lannan Foundation Fellowship.

关于译者

方美昂女士是北卡罗莱纳大学 (University of North Carolina) 卡罗莱纳表演艺术中心的行政与艺术总监。此前曾在中国工作、生活长达二十年。方美昂女士曾担任香港西九文化区的表演艺术总监。西九文化区是全球最具规模的艺术与文化发展机构之一。在此之前，方美昂女士曾创立联结中国与国际文化交流机构"乒乓策划"，并担任其总裁。历年来，方美昂女士策划的艺术文化项目遍及全球五大洲五十多个国家。方美昂女士曾作为2002-03年富布赖特奖学金学者赴中国北京大学及北京舞蹈学院进行学术研究，并曾是肯尼迪艺术中心表演艺术管理研习班成员。

About the Poetry Translator

Alison M. Friedman has served as the James and Susan Moeser executive and artistic director for Carolina Performing Arts at UNC Chapel Hill since 2021 and as the Chancellor's Arts Advisor since 2025. Previously, Friedman was artistic director of performing arts for West Kowloon Cultural District in Hong Kong, one of the world's largest arts and cultural developments. Before that, she founded and ran Ping Pong Productions, a US- and Beijing-registered cultural exchange organization that worked in more than 50 countries on five continents. Fluent in Mandarin, she is a fellow at the National Committee on U.S.-China Relations Public Intellectual Program, and was a 2002-03 Fulbright Scholar to China.